The Well Fed

Baby

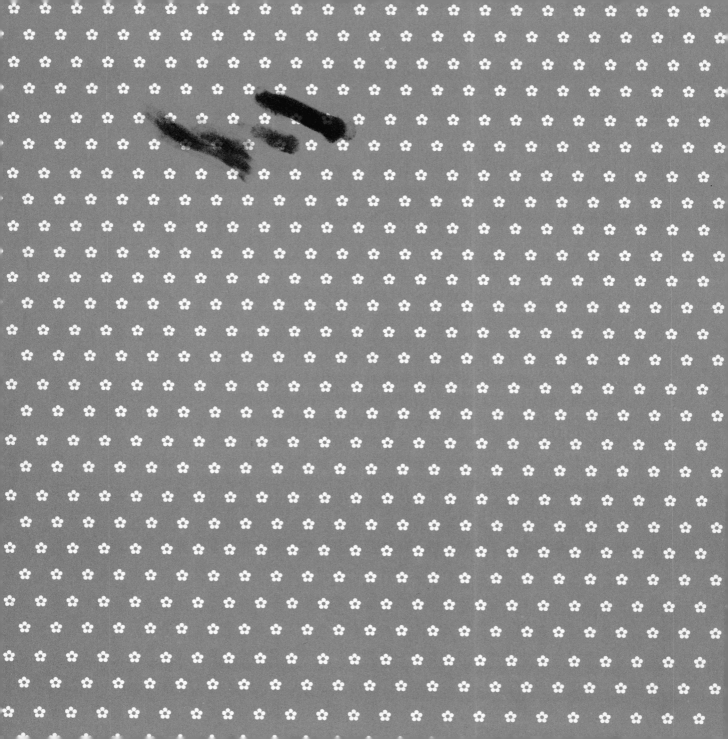

The Well Fed Baby

O. ROBIN SWEET AND THOMAS A. BLOOM, PH.D.

William Morrow and Company, Inc.
New York

Library of Congress Cataloging-in-Publication Data

Sweet, O. Robin.
   The well fed baby : O. Robin Sweet and Thomas A. Bloom.
     p. cm.
   Includes index.
   ISBN 0-688-17823-5
   1. Infants—Nutrition.   2. Baby foods.   3. Cookery (Baby foods)
I. Title.   II. Bloom,Thomas A.
RJ216.S923 2000
613.2'083'221—dc21   99-044185

Printed in the United States of America

First Edition

        4   5   6   7   8   9   10

BOOK DESIGN BY RENATO STANISIC

www.williammorrow.com

In June 1992, we traveled to St. Petersburg (Leningrad), Russia, to adopt a baby. Upon our arrival, we located an orphanage and found a six-month-old boy whom we adopted and named Nikolai.

Nikolai weighed only six pounds when we found him and was suffering from pneumonia. He also had rickets (a severe dietary and vitamin deficiency). His total daily food intake consisted of room-temperature tea with sugar and a syrup-laden powdered dairy substitute. He had a distended stomach, and it was obvious that he was suffering from severe malnutrition.

After a healthy diet consisting of soy-based formula, infant vitamins, organic cereal/grains, fresh vegetables, and fruit, Nikolai is a healthy seven-year-old weighing in at sixty-five pounds and over four feet tall.

Nikolai's recovery and weight gain are due solely to proper nutrition and care (lots of love). To celebrate this remarkable recovery, we decided to write a book entitled The Well Fed Baby, which we dedicate to our son, Josef Nikolai Bloom, and to his two sisters who adore him, Gretchen and Alexis.

CONTENTS

❀

Foreword

BY DALE V. ATKINS, PH.D.

What do babies need? Not a difficult question, but think about it for a moment. They need love, nurturing, gentleness, safety—and all from people who respond to their needs tenderly, in a comfortable, predictable, responsive environment.

Babies develop a sense of themselves, their value, in large measure by the manner in which their caregivers interact with them. Smiles; playfulness; sweet voice tones; unhurried, patient speech and actions, all combine to create an atmosphere that conveys caring.

A great deal of our interaction with baby centers on food. And since babies thrive on good, wholesome, healthy food, why not learn the best, easiest ways to prepare food that nurtures their developing minds and bodies, and spirits. We know what it takes to nourish our children. With a healthy start your baby will reap benefits his or her whole life.

Another simple question: Is there really such a thing as "comfort" food? Yes, indeed there is. Comfort foods are created in secure, happy atmospheres reminiscent of those times when favorite relatives came to visit and special meals were prepared. We associate certain foods with good feelings and the wonderful aromas that would waft through the house from the kitchen. For most of us, these images evoke warm feelings and true nourishment for the body and soul. For so many of us, the family recipe books and boxes bring to mind delightful thoughts and conversations about the good, delectable times.

Seeing the dramatic impact that healthy food, lovingly prepared and served with smiles, can have on a child's development, we must sit up and take notice. And what better way to learn about nutrition and the various ways to prepare grains, fruits, vegetables, all types of foods, than to learn from the finest chefs in the country? O. Robin Sweet and Dr. Thomas Bloom offer their invaluable expertise drawn from a lifetime of work in the fields of pediatrics, nutrition, and food preparation. They know health. Additionally, they learned the necessity of feeding nutritious foods to their young son, Nikolai, in order to literally save his life. He thrived as a result of their dedicated, knowledgeable efforts.

Most of us do not face such extreme situations, but why not feed our children what is best for them so they can thrive? By writing this wonderful book, Robin and Tom have given us all a priceless gift. I heartily recommend *The Well-Fed Baby*. It belongs on every family's book shelf, within easy reach. Enjoy!

Dr. Dale Atkins is a noted New York child psychologist, author of numerous books on parenting and children's health, and host of the Mothering *television show.*

Baby's Introduction to Eating

❀

With more than 4 million births each year in the United States alone, it amazes us that more value has not been placed on infant nutrition and education. In this edition, we plan to reinforce introducing healthy foods right from the start.

Since we authored the first edition of this book, we have formed The Well Fed Baby Company, which manufactures the first line of frozen, organic, kosher, soy-based baby food. Why, you ask? The reader response from the initial publication of this cookbook was so tremendous, consumer demand forced us into production. The majority of parents want the best for their babies and often do not have the time, energy, or desire to prepare baby's meals from scratch. In this new edition, we are hoping to share our company's philosophy, which is focused on the benefits of organics, soy foods, and initiating healthy eating habits from birth.

There has been much consumer awareness through media coverage of the benefits of consuming organic and soy foods as adults, but not so much focus on those same benefits for infants and children. In Dr. Benjamin Spock's new seventh edition of *Baby and Child Care*, he advises parents to provide an all-plant, or vegan, diet for their children. Spock's recommendation would mean relying on vegetables, fortified plant foods and drinks, and a daily vitamin-mineral supplement to provide needed amounts of essential nutrients like calcium, iron, zinc, and vitamins D and B_{12} that are most readily available from soy-based foods.

The vegan diet is so healthful because you avoid the saturated fats and cholesterol in animal foods. You also consume lots of fiber and nutrients from vegetables and fruits, which go a long way in reducing problems with heart disease, obesity, high blood pressure, gallbladder disease, and some cancer-related disease later in life.

In its current *Pediatric Nutrition Handbook*, the Academy of Pediatrics points out that small children can do very well on a diet that is partly vegetarian (includes no red meats or poultry, but does include fish, dairy products, eggs, and plants) or lacto-vegetarian with dairy products as the only animal products. For vegans, however, the academy says parents must pay close attention to what their children eat to be sure that a wide variety of food is consumed and that meals are nutritionally balanced. It urges particular care in making sure vegan children get enough of certain nutrients that other children get from animal foods.

Parents generally have the most profound and lasting influence on their children's eating habits and food tolerances. To a large extent, these tolerances and habits are influenced by how babies are introduced to foods, how we promote good eating habits, and how we educate them about food. This educational process involves more than just teaching them good versus bad, such as avoiding sugar, fat, cholesterol, sodium, and so on, and emphasizing fruits and vegetables. The educational process should include introducing children to a wide range of tastes and textures, without a preordained dichotomy between "foods that are good for you" and "foods that taste good."

Today, most adults are aware and firmly convinced that natural foods surpass processed foods in both flavor and nutritional value. These same adults know that diet and health are inextricably linked, and therefore have altered the way they eat and cook. Unfortunately, these realizations have not always filtered down to the way we feed our youngest eaters.

We often fail to associate infant nutrition with adult nutrition, thinking that infant nutrition is somehow removed or distant from our own notions of healthy eating. Consciously or unconsciously, most parents associate the feeding of infants, six months to one year, with the purchase of costly, multicolored little jars, with each color representing variety. With confidence and trust, we place the nutritional responsibility and diet of our children in the hands of baby food manufacturers who often charge high prices for processed foods that can be made naturally at home in just minutes at a fraction of the cost.

The Well Fed Baby presents an enjoyable, economical, and sound system of preparing nutritious foods for babies. It reflects the expertise of the two authors: O. Robin Sweet is a pediatric nurse and expert on health and prenatal and toddler care, and president of The Well Fed Baby, Inc. Dr. Thomas A. Bloom is a trained chef, consultant in food science, past president of the California Culinary Academy, and vice-president of the Culinary Institute of America.

The recipes originate from professional chefs and other food professionals whose cooking philosophies focus on using natural ingredients to prepare nutritional, well-balanced meals. These individuals do not bring an elitist approach to the book. Rather, they have fully embraced national and international nutritional concerns, and address them on a daily basis in both their professional kitchens and their kitchens at home.

These chefs understand food values as well as flavors and textures, and are dedicated to the principle that food, while necessary to sustain life and assure proper growth, is also a joy, a ritual, and a binding force between (in this case) babies and their families. Most of the chefs who have contributed recipes have babies and/or small children, and their recipes reflect both their personal and professional work with baby food. Each recipe is intended to be unique; simple, not fancy, easy to make, economical, delicious, and nutritious. In all, they represent real food for real small eaters.

This is a unique cookbook designed to add a special flair to the diet of infants. The book teaches adults all they need to know about how to introduce babies to solid foods: which foods to avoid for allergic reactions, early tolerances, quantities (portion control), and dietary balances to assure proper nutrition. All recipes are economical to prepare and nutritionally sound for children six to twelve months of age. Each chapter focuses on a meal period, including breakfast, lunch, dinner, and snacks. The recipes are presented in a way so that they may be easily prepared. A registered dietician has conducted an analysis of each recipe for its nutritional value (calories, saturated fat, sodium, cholesterol, iron, protein, and carbohydrates), which is unique to this cookbook.

Healthy eating is one of the most important things we can do for ourselves and our children. Most pediatricians recommend that solid foods not be included in infant's daily diet until they are six months of age. They have found that the protein, fat, and carbohydrate content of breast milk and formula are nutritionally complete and properly balanced for babies, whereas the addition of solid foods changes this natural balance and may tend to promote food allergies. The early introduction of solids often increases the possibility of infants developing allergies as well as increasing the sodium content of their diet. This may eventually contribute to high blood pressure or obesity later in life. Solid foods also interfere with the absorption of iron in breast milk. Contrary to popular belief, solids do not help babies sleep through the night. Also, physically, before six months of age, your baby does not have the digestive system capable of processing solid foods nor the motor development to eat them, because the baby's tongue and cheek muscles have only been used for sucking. Therefore, by holding off on solids, you are allowing your baby's motor development and immature digestive system time to grow ready for other foods. After a half-year of being strengthened with breast milk/formula, most children's digestive systems are mature enough to start drawing nutrients from other foods. Your baby may be ready for solids at about six months of age or more. Active babies may require solid foods a month earlier, while others refuse to swallow anything until they walk. If your baby is chewing toys out of hunger, which only a parent can tell, rather than for relief of sore, teething gums, or is eyeing your lunch, then it may also be time for solid foods.

According to the Academy of Pediatrics, six months can be an important age for a baby's nutritional needs. The iron supply that mothers give to the child before birth is nearly gone, so extra nutrients may be needed. In this age of low-fat and fat-free diets, some parents incorrectly believe that their babies should be placed on such a diet immediately. What most parents do not realize is that babies need fat for healthy brain development, and the majority of pediatricians feel that low-fat diets are not recommended for babies under two years of age.

SOY FOODS

There are many health benefits associated with the consumption of soy, but the main body of information focuses on four subjects: heart disease, cancer, osteoporosis, and menopause. Soy has also been linked to the prevention of hormone-induced cancers including colon, liver, prostate, and lung, and some forms of leukemia.

Aside from the known health benefits associated with eliminating animal protein from one's diet, research suggests that the phytochemicals in soy are powerful substances that can affect cancer, heart disease, and menopause—even diabetes. Soy products contain enough vitamins, minerals, amino acids, protein, fiber, and calcium to sustain health.

Not all soy products are created equal. Soy sauce and soybean oils do not contain isoflavones. Other soy products may be fortified with vitamins and/or calcium, yet drinking calcium-enriched soy will not do any more to prevent osteoporosis than drinking soy that has not been calcium-enriched.

Soy milk is the fastest-growing segment of soy food sales, and its new mass market availability contributes to its popularity. Many grocers are carrying soy milks in the dairy case—providing a convenient resource for consumers that also forces the uninitiated to make a connection between soy milk and cow's milk. Soy milk should not be used as a substitute for infant formula or breast milk. We recommend it in the preparation of any and all recipes that call for milk or cream.

Meat analogs incorporating soy protein are growing in popularity as well. These include soy burgers, hot dogs and sausages—even battered "chicken" strips. Currently soybeans are sold in frozen vegetable mixes. Soy "cream cheese," "yogurt" spreads, and "butter" alternatives are readily available. Soy "cheeses" that taste like Cheddar and mozzarella are available in slices. Soy nut butter is gaining recognition; it is even being used in school cafeterias in deference to children with peanut allergies.

When preparing and/or storing food for your infant/toddler, you should be knowledgeable about food-borne illnesses such as staphylococcus, salmonella, and botulism. We recommend preparing most recipes for one meal only. In most cases, fresh seasonal food is best. If packaged foods are used, labels should be checked and those with high salt and sugar contents should be avoided. If you do have leftovers, place the food in a clean container, leave the lid off until the food comes to room temperature, and then put the lid on and place it in the refrigerator. Another option is to cool the food quickly by putting it in a shallow pan and placing the pan in an ice bath; then place the food into a clean, dry container with a lock top and freeze immediately. Freezing is recommended for storing foods longer than forty-eight hours, but do not keep food in the freezer for more than one month. Foods may be frozen in ice cube trays or small airtight containers so that individual servings can be heated and used one at a time. Labeling and dating of all frozen foods is advisable. To clean the cooking utensils before and after use, please scrub all equipment with soap and hot water and rinse well. If you feel the need to sanitize the equipment, you must place the utensils in 212°F (boiling) water, or use a sanitizer. Clean means free from food soil or dirt. Sanitary means free of germs. Some dishwashers actually have a "sani-cycle," which is an easy, convenient way to sanitize.

Baby foods may be prepared using a food processor, electric blender, or food mill, or by mashing with a fork. The food that you have prepared for one meal should not be reused if you have put the spoon from the baby's mouth back into the dish of food. The bacteria from his saliva could contaminate the remaining food. Discard any leftovers from the dish.

THE IMPORTANCE OF ORGANICS

Organic farming is a production system that avoids the use of synthetically compounded fertilizers, pesticides, growth regulators, and livestock feed additives. To the maximum extent feasible, organic farming systems rely on crop rotations, crop residues, animal manures, legumes, green manures, off-the-farm organic wastes, mechanical cultivation, mineral-bearing rocks, and aspects of biological pest control to maintain soil productivity and tilth; to supply plant nutrients; and to control insects, weeds, and other pests.

This approach to agriculture brings us inevitably to an understanding that what we eat, and how those things are grown, affect all of the planet in a profound way.

The culinary director of Fetzer's Food and Wine Center, John Ash, is a steadfast supporter of organics and adds that "one cannot dine well unless one has chosen their food responsibly and in a way that recognizes that we are stewards of the earth and all that lives on it. This is the importance of organic agriculture."

FOOD ALLERGIES

Food allergies develop when a food triggers a reaction in the baby's immune system and the body reacts to the food as a harmful substance. Allergic reactions vary in degree. The gastrointestinal tract can be affected, and your baby may have cramps, diarrhea, vomiting and/or nausea. The respiratory system may react to a food by causing wheezing, coughing, sneezing, runny nose, or shortness of breath. Skin reactions may include a rash, hives, or swelling of the lips or around the eyes. The symptoms of an allergy may occur immediately, within a few minutes, after a few hours, or sometimes not for forty-eight hours. We recommend that if you notice any of these symptoms after feeding your baby a specific food, you contact your pediatrician. Some of the foods most likely to cause allergic reactions include: cow's milk, egg whites, peanuts, soybeans, shellfish, wheat, peas, beans, and certain spices. If your family has a history of allergies, monitor your baby's reaction to pork, fish, nuts, cabbage, corn, tomatoes, citrus juice, onions, wheat, rye, yeast, chocolate, and all berries. While most babies won't have an allergic reaction to these foods, you must introduce them slowly, and look for any unusual reactions.

THINGS TO AVOID

Anything artificially colored, high in sugar, fat, preservatives, salt, or adulterated with additives is not good for your baby. The only sweetener you should be using is natural fruit juice. The natural sugars found in fruit, vegetables, grains, and breast milk are necessary to our diets and are processed efficiently. Added sweeteners, including natural sweeteners, refined sugar, and artificial sweeteners are empty calories and crowd out the foods your baby really needs. However, it is necessary to use sugar in some of our recipes, but the amount of sugar per serving is minimal. Avoid foods high in sodium, such as bacon, potato chips, ham, pickles, deli foods, salt, sausages, and smoked foods. Avoid foods high in fat, such as chocolate, coconut oil, croissants, fatty foods, fried foods, margarine (more than the recommended daily allowance), nuts, pastry, and salad dressings. Avoid processed foods or foods high in sugar, such as candy, cakes, canned fruit (check the label to see if it is packaged in fruit juice as opposed to syrup), flavored drinks, processed cheese, marinated cherries (red dye), condiments (catsup, mustard, mayonnaise, relish), prepackaged cookies, diabetic foods (saccharin is added to some and has been found to be carcinogenic), doughnuts, gelatins, hot dogs, instant foods, jams, jellies, processed meats, and pie. Avoid the following miscellaneous foods: citrus fruits (too acidic in the first year of life), coffee, egg whites, honey, rye bread, white bread, and strawberries.

Avoid the following foods because they are not completely digestable by babies under two years of age and are known to cause choking: nuts, hot dogs, popcorn, grapes, sunflower seeds or seeds of any kind, uncooked carrots, and corn.

A NOTE ABOUT HONEY

Never feed your baby honey or use it to coat a pacifier during the first year. Honey may contain spores of bacteria that can cause infant botulism and affect the baby's nerves and muscles, and can be fatal. Symptoms of this disease include weakness, constipation, and poor appetite. These bacteria can grow in the infant's intestine and become a strong poison. It is possible that raw fruits, raw vegetables, and corn syrups (light and dark) may also contain the botulism spores. To be safe, follow the advice of your pediatrician. If your baby develops this problem, he may need to be treated in a hospital. Almost all babies with this disease recover fully, if treated in time. After one year of age, babies generally no longer get sick from eating honey. We have included recipes that use honey, but they are cooked/baked items, which don't transmit the botulism.

TEETH

Avoid giving your baby fruit juice or milk in a bottle, and then putting him to bed. Milk or juice will pool in the baby's mouth, which will promote tooth decay even before she has teeth! It is also not wise to feed her anything sweet before bedtime, as this coats the mouth with sugar. It is very important that, as soon as your baby has even one tooth, you brush it/them, at least once a day. Use a baby toothbrush or a clean piece of gauze to wipe her teeth/tooth after every meal. Tooth decay is caused by an excess of sugar, so watch your baby's diet.

ESSENTIAL EQUIPMENT

You will need the following furniture, kitchen equipment, and utensils in order to feed your baby.
- sturdy highchair (try to get a tray with a lip) or clamp-on seat (make sure that you always strap your baby into the seat.)
- nonbreakable bowl and small nonbreakable spoon (coated with a soft plastic, which is preferable for baby's sensitive gums)
- bibs, the jumbo/wipe-off type, or diapers or washcloths
- apron for you
- plastic baby cup (with lid)
- sharp knives to chop foods
- vegetable scrubbing brush for washing produce
- peelers for fruits and vegetables

- vegetable steamer
- small saucepans for cooking/heating tiny portions
- spatula with handle to scrape sides of blender
- an old shower curtain or sheet to place underneath the highchair area, or you can purchase square plastic protectors at most juvenile stores
- baby food grinder (portable tool for purees), blender (to puree chunky family foods), or food processor

GENERAL GUIDELINES FOR FEEDING BABY

- If you are still nursing, nurse your baby before feedings, or offer formula. This is the most important food at this time, so if baby fills up on milk and only takes a little bit of food, this is nutritionally acceptable.
- Start with one food, a teaspoon at a time, for three days or so. Watch for allergies before adding other foods.
- General rule for pureeing or simmering: one tablespoon of water or breast milk or formula per whole piece of fresh fruit or vegetable.
- General rule for freezing: Cook and puree two tablespoons of water/breast milk or formula and two whole pieces of fruit or vegetable, and fill the individual slots of an ice cube tray. Cover and freeze. About an hour before feeding baby, remove as many cubes as you need and let them thaw to room temperature. Try to use them soon after thawing. Don't refreeze any food, and throw away leftovers.
- Best cooking methods: steaming, poaching, or baking. Avoid canned and commercially frozen food, if possible; at the very least, rinse off any salt or sweet syrup.
- Vegetables and fruits: Wash thoroughly and peel to remove any trace of herbicides or pesticides from the skin. Start with lightly steamed yellow squash and other

more bland vegetables before adding the sweeter taste of fruits such as organically grown banana. Mash for spoon feeding, or finely chop for finger feeding.

- Children's food generally should not have a high flavor profile, so don't add seasonings and spices. Please introduce intense flavors gradually.
- Never leave a baby unattended with food. Children can choke very easily on the smallest of pieces.

HOW TO STRAIN FOOD

It is very important to strain your baby's first foods. Without your realizing it, many foods that have been pureed still contain bits of skin that can cause choking. Once your baby has mastered the art of eating a thicker-consistency food, it is safe to strain food at your discretion. You can purchase a strainer at any discount store, cooking store, or even at children's shops. Most strainers (except for a tea strainer) have the same type of mesh that is adequate for straining baby foods.

To strain cooked, pureed foods, simply spoon approximately one tablespoon at a time into a strainer and then, with the back of a wooden (our preference but not necessary) spoon, in a circular motion, gently press the food through the strainer, making sure that you do not press too hard, which would allow the skin to pass through.

RECOMMENDED DIETARY ALLOWANCES

Recommended dietary allowances are defined as food substances, liquid and solid, regularly consumed in the course of normal living. A prescribed allowance of food adapted for a particular age group is adequate in energy-providing substances (carbohydrates and fats), tissue-building substances (proteins), inorganic substances (water and mineral salts), regulating substances (vitamins), and substances that promote physiological processes (such as bulk for promoting peristaltic movements in the digestive tract). The chart below lists the recommended daily dietary allowances for children up to three years of age.

CHILD'S WEIGHT UP TO 29 POUNDS
Energy (calories): 900 to 1,800
Protein: 23 grams

FAT SOLUBLE VITAMINS
Vitamin A: 400 micrograms
Vitamin D: 10 micrograms
Vitamin E: 5 milligrams

WATER SOLUBLE VITAMINS
Ascorbic acid: 45 milligrams
Folacin: 100 micrograms
Niacin: 9 milligrams
Riboflavin: 0.8 milligrams
Thiamin: 0.7 milligrams
Vitamin B_6: 0.9 milligrams
Vitamin B_{12}: 2 micrograms

MINERALS

Calcium: 800 milligrams
Phosphorus: 800 milligrams
Iodine: 70 micrograms
Iron: 15 milligrams
Magnesium: 150 milligrams
Zinc: 10 milligrams

Sources of Vitamin A

Apricots
Broccoli
Cantaloupe
Carrots
Cooked greens
Pumpkin
Squash
Sweet potatoes

Sources of Vitamin C

Cabbage
Cantaloupe
Green pepper
Guava
Citrus fruits

Strawberries
Tomatoes
Watermelon

Sources of Vitamin D

Chances are that your pediatrician will already have your baby on a multivitamin. Vitamin D is a hormone formed in the body by the action of the sunlight. There is very little vitamin D in breast milk or cow's milk. The best source of vitamin D is the sunlight. It takes only fifteen minutes a day, even with your baby fully clothed, for him to get the daily allowance. The sun on your baby's hands and face will do the job.

In summary, we hope to inform parents of the importance of infant and child nutrition and to provide information regarding:

1. how and when to introduce new foods to babies and small children
2. how to provide a variety of healthy, well-balanced snacks and meals
3. how to identify and avoid food allergies
4. how to prepare meals that babies and small children can eat.

Bon appétit!

1

❀

Feeding the Well Fed Baby

THE FEEDING AND DIET REQUIREMENTS OF BABIES AND toddlers vary significantly with age. This chapter addresses these dietary requirements by presenting month-by-month general feeding and diet guidelines for babies and toddlers six months through twelve months of age, as well as information on specific foods for babies with teeth. Baby's first bites should be diluted, just slightly thicker than breast milk or formula. Gradually increase the thickness of the mixture and the portion size as your baby becomes more accustomed to eating. We recommend beginning with cereal, then adding strained vegetables, then fruit, and, finally, meat. Within two or three months after your baby starts solids, his diet can consist of all of the above, distributed among three meals a day. Some parents are concerned about feeding a baby too much, but a healthy baby will stop eating when he's full.

6 months: milk, cereal (strained)

7 to 8 months: milk, cereal, juice, vegetables, tofu, soy food, and fruit (pureed)

8 to 10 months: meat (coarsely pureed or finely minced)

10 to 12 months: chopped foods

12 to 36 months: cut as tolerated

FIRST FOODS

When feeding your baby, place the spoon on the top of her tongue when feeding, and let her suck the food off the spoon. Make sure that the consistency of the food is almost liquid, otherwise she will gag. Use soft-coated spoons so as not to irritate baby's sensitive gums.

Hint: It is much easier to feed a baby when his hands are occupied. We have multiple washable toys by the highchair that we use at every mealtime!

Every baby is different, so the amounts of fruit, formula, and cereal that we recommend are estimates. Use trial and error with your baby. We believe in pureeing one whole piece of fruit and using it in the cereal in the morning, then with tofu for lunch and dinner. When making more food, it is better to have too much than too little when your baby is fussy and still hungry. Once your baby's appetite increases, one whole piece of fruit will most likely be consumed at lunch. There is also no defined time to add foods that have more texture. We find that it depends on the individual baby. Usually, you can offer "lumpier" foods when your baby has two top teeth and two bottom teeth. Up until this point, he doesn't have the teeth to grind the food into smaller pieces, so offer different foods gradually. Your baby will let you know whether or not he is ready for more advanced foods. The most obvious sign that he is *not* ready is gagging, choking, or just spitting the food out.

We believe in warming all baby foods to just above lukewarm temperature. Please test all foods before offering them to your baby. Microwave ovens make the food extremely hot in the middle, so the temperature on the outside is deceiving. In all of the recipes, we have used formula for the liquid ingredient; however, if you have expressed breast milk handy, please use it in place of formula. If you are a nursing mother and you do not have breast milk available, use a soy-based formula. We have found that the chance of an adverse reaction is less likely, but please consult with your pediatrician.

We are very fortunate in California as we have a wide selection of fresh produce available throughout the year. However, this is not so for the majority of the country, so we asked our contributing chefs what they would recommend as an alternative. They suggested using frozen vegetables and fruits due to the quality and freshness when frozen and the fact that most of these foods' vitamins are still intact. When you are shopping for fruit and produce, look for the very freshest, as products that have been left on the shelves for days will have lost flavor and vitamins.

FEEDING BABIES SIX MONTHS OF AGE

- Keep breast milk or formula as the priority food for the first year.
- Provide breast milk on request (at least five feedings every twenty-four hours) or formula (24 to 32 ounces every twenty-four hours).
- Give vitamins and minerals only if prescribed by your doctor.
- Solid foods, such as cereal, generally should not be started until your baby is six months old. If you choose to introduce cereals to your baby's diet before then, remember that possible allergic reactions such as diarrhea, vomiting, coughing, and/or rashes may occur. To avoid these reactions, most pediatricians recommend starting your child's first solids with a bland single-grain cereal, such as rice, oat, or barley, moistened with water or breast milk. Wait until seven to nine months to

introduce wheat, mixed cereals, high-protein cereals, and cooked Cream of Wheat. First solids should consist of the purest and most nutritious foods available. Not only are you introducing your baby to the taste of food, but you are also attempting to provide the vitamins, minerals, natural fats, and other properties of breast milk.

- When you first introduce your baby to cereal, it is recommended to mix 1 tablespoon of cereal with 2 to 3 tablespoons of breast milk or formula. Make it thin. As she gets older, you can make the cereal thicker and increase the portion to 3 tablespoons of cereal plus milk. Do not add sugar. Feed a very small amount; about ⅛ teaspoon at a time, slowly increasing the amount as she is able to handle it.
- At first your baby may appear to push the cereal back out of her mouth. This does not necessarily mean she does not like it; she is developing the ability to use her tongue to swallow. Your baby is now developing a new set of muscles that were not used in breastfeeding/bottlefeeding. Nursing infants use their tongue to press the breast's nipple against the top of their mouth. This sucking reflex will actually push the solid food out of their mouth. It is important to understand that when a baby does not want any more to eat, she will angrily turn her head away or spit the food all over you. Do not make a habit of pushing or forcing one more bite, as this may start overeating habits.
- Do not feed cereal in the bottle with milk. Feed from a spoon. This helps the tongue muscle development, which in turn helps promote clearer speech patterns later on.
- It is best not to add salt, sugar, pepper, or seasonings to your baby's foods. It is not necessary for a baby's diet nor is it recommended by the American Dietetic Association.

When your baby is six months of age, you may start with your everyday, home-cooked whole foods. Not only will you spare yourself the tremendous expense of processed baby foods, but your baby will become accustomed to the taste of different foods.

As your baby develops more teeth, he will be able to enjoy a greater selection of solid foods and will make an easy transition to enjoying whatever you are eating.

At six months old, some babies are ready to plunge right into finger feeding. To help your baby, simply place small bits of food on the highchair tray or on an unbreakable plate.

If he seems too young for anything but spoon feeding, try holding him on your lap and gently letting a tiny bit of food slip from the spoon into his mouth.

Perfect First Foods

Most babies enjoy certain foods over other foods. The following are foods that are nutritionally sound and safe for your baby at six months of age:

whole-grain toast (crusts of bread), bagels, or unsweetened cereal

whole-grain rice, oats, or barley (mashed or served as cereal)

Terrific Teething Foods

At six months of age, many babies begin teething and need foods that both feel good on the gums and meet nutritional requirements.

Bread crusts: Well-toasted, whole-grain bread and bagels are great for teething. You can save "heels" in the refrigerator; chilled crusts or bagels are often rock hard and nicely cold on baby's gums.

Carrots: Make sure it's a nice fat one, and has been cleaned and peeled. Carrot sticks are too small and a teething baby might break them into small, chokeable pieces. If the baby is teething, place the carrot in the freezer for a while, and the coldness will feel wonderful on his sore gums.

FEEDING BABIES SEVEN MONTHS OF AGE

- Provide breast milk on request (approximately five feedings every twenty-four hours) or formula (24 to 32 ounces).
- Give vitamins and minerals only if prescribed by your pediatrician.
- Your baby is now ready for cereal mixed with pureed fruits, and vegetables.
- You may now introduce other cereals including high-protein cereals and Cream of Wheat (4 to 6 tablespoons of dry cereal mixed with 2 to 4 ounces of breast milk or formula).
- Introduce new foods one at a time, including such foods as pureed/mashed fruits and vegetables. Begin with 1 tablespoon and gradually increase the amount given to 4 tablespoons (as tolerated).
- When you introduce a new food to your baby's diet, wait three days before introducing another. If an allergic reaction such as a rash, vomiting, or diarrhea should occur, it will then be easy to determine which new food caused the problem.
- Giving your baby a larger amount of a single food at a feeding, rather than small amounts of several foods, allows her to get used to a new food so that she will be less likely to reject it. She is also less likely to have an allergic reaction, because her body has to handle only one new food item at a time.

Cereals

Iron is important because by this time your baby's iron stores are used up, and infants need iron so that the brain will develop properly. Over a period of time, babies can learn to accept different tastes and textures and learn to feed themselves while also developing chewing skills. Once he has mastered the technique of eating cereal, you can add foods with a coarser texture and stronger taste to the cereal, such as squash, sweet potatoes, or green beans. Mixing pureed cooked vegetables or beans with cereal provides excellent nutritious food until he is ready for chunky, chewy foods such as broccoli or cooked carrots.

Preparing Your Baby's Cereal

- At seven months she is better able to digest the cereal, and you can gradually thicken it by adding more cereal to the liquid.
- Every three days, she should be ready for a new cereal and a new taste experience. A good order is a rice cereal, then oatmeal, then a barley cereal. If you use a dry cereal, you must soak it thoroughly until it is soft, then dilute it to the right consistency.

Vegetables

Once your baby is eating cereals, at about seven months of age, he should be ready to try vegetables. Pediatricians recommend that you introduce vegetables first rather than sweet fruits, to reduce the tendency to develop a sweet tooth. Start with pureed or strained green beans and peas, pumpkin, squash, and potatoes (both sweet and white). Then your baby will be ready for chewy vegetables; try zucchini, broccoli, cauliflower, asparagus tips, and kale. Don't feed him pureed spinach, beets, turnips, carrots, or collard greens until at least nine months of age, as these vegetables may be too rich in nitrates.

Soy Food

Tofu (soybean curd) is a wonderful protein substitute for meat, which infants have a tendency to reject. We have included various recipes that include tofu in both the Lunch and Dinner chapters. Tempeh is another soy food produced by a natural aging process. Tempeh, like yogurt, is a live food whose active enzymes make it easily digestible. It also is the best vegetarian source of vitamin B_{12} currently known. Tempeh is as versatile a food as tofu and has a distinctly meatier taste and texture.

Fruit Juice

When he is around seven months of age, noncitrus fruit juice is a welcome addition to the baby's diet. Dilute fruit juice with water (two parts to one) at first, because baby's digestive system is very sensitive, or use baby juices. Use strained fresh, canned, or frozen juices. If the juice does not come prestrained, then use a very fine sieve. Start with apple, pear, or peach juice/nectars. We recommend using the bottled infant juices due to their purity and lack of pesticides. Some apple juices on the market still use apples that were sprayed with alar, which infant juices do not use. Do not give citrus juices until your baby is one year old to prevent possible allergies. Do not give artificially flavored fruit drinks such as punch or soda. These are often lacking in nutrients. To start, simply offer 2 ounces (4 tablespoons) of fruit juice and 1 ounce (2 tablespoons) of water mixed together in a small plastic cup that has a covered top and a drinking spout, or in a baby bottle. Gradually increase to 4 to 8 ounces (½ to 1 cup) of juice every twenty-four hours.

Fruits

About a month (seven to eight months of age) after introducing vegetables to your baby's diet, she should be ready to eat noncitrus fruits. Start with cooked fruit, which is softer and easier to puree; it is easiest to bake it. Preheat the oven to 350°F, wash the fruit, bake it in its skin (pierce the fruit's skin with a fork to make sure that it does not explode in the oven) in a covered dish with just a little water. When it's tender, it is done. Apples, peaches, apricots, pears, nectarines, papayas, and plums are recommended. Avoid fresh (non-organically grown) bananas, as their porous skin admits the toxic fungicides that must be sprayed on all imported fruits. If you want to serve your baby bananas, purchase organically grown bananas. Feed your baby only fruits that are in season (it is more economical and your baby is getting fresh as opposed to canned fruits) and that are washed or peeled. Buy local, ripened, organically grown fruits if possible. After your child has mastered eating cooked fruit, introduce uncooked mashed fruit to her diet, as the natural texture will help her learn to chew.

FEEDING BABIES EIGHT MONTHS OF AGE

As your baby matures, you may begin to introduce new foods as well as increase the amount of food.

- Provide breast milk or formula on demand (four to five feedings every twenty-four hours, or 24 to 32 ounces of formula).
- Continue to feed him cereal (4 to 6 tablespoons a day).
- Continue to feed him vegetables, cooked or pureed (4 tablespoons a day).
- Continue to feed him fruit, cooked, pureed, or fresh (4 tablespoons a day).
- Most pediatricians recommend introducing fluoridated water at this time (3 to 4 ounces a day in hot weather or as desired). Most babies tend to choke on and spit out water only because it is a thinner liquid than they are accustomed to.
- Give vitamins and minerals only if prescribed by your doctor.
- You may now introduce hard-boiled egg yolks. Use the yolk only. Mash the hard-boiled yolk with a fork and mix with a little breast milk, formula, and/or infant cereal. It is not wise to include egg whites in the diet before the first year as there is a risk of promoting allergies. However, using egg whites when you are baking is fine. Begin with one teaspoon of egg yolk and gradually increase until the whole

yolk is eaten. We recommend hard-boiling eggs, which kills the bacteria salmonella that can cause mild gastroenteritis (upset stomach). Other salmonella strains have been known to cause fatal food poisoning. Please cook all eggs until they are well done.

- Cottage cheese and plain low-fat yogurt may also be offered at eight months. Begin with one teaspoon and gradually increase to 2 to 4 tablespoons. Yogurt is more digestible than cow's milk, and adds beneficial lactobacillus organisms to the baby's intestinal tract. You can mix fresh fruit with it, but stay away from the commercial, high-sugar yogurt with fruit combinations. Many contain preservatives, so please read the label carefully. Sheep's yogurt is another wonderful option. However, it may be difficult to locate in your local grocery, but try health food stores or local farms. Your child may enjoy plain yogurt all her life if she acquires a taste for it now.

- Lean, well-cooked meat, finely strained or pureed, can also be introduced at this age to provide protein. Begin with 1 teaspoon and gradually increase to 4 tablespoons. Start with poultry, then beef, then lamb. Purees of soft-cooked beans and lentils (strained though a sieve) are a good substitute for meat, and may be given in the same amount.

- Teething foods like unsalted soda crackers and graham crackers can now be offered. Close supervision is necessary, however, to prevent the possibility of choking.

- Remember that breast milk or formula is still the most important food for your baby at this age. Therefore, the amount of food should not be so great that he refuses the usual amount of breast milk or formula (24 ounces per twenty-four hours, at least).

FEEDING BABIES NINE MONTHS OF AGE

Now you may begin to introduce new foods to your baby's diet as well as increase the quantity of food.

- Provide breast milk on demand (at least three to five feedings every twenty-four hours) or formula (24 to 32 ounces).
- Give plain water as needed.
- Give vitamins and minerals only if prescribed by a doctor.
- Continue to feed your baby cereal (4 tablespoons of cereal mixed with breast milk, formula, fruit or fruit juice). Introduce other more advanced infant cereals such as wheat, mixed grain, and high protein.
- Continue to feed your baby vegetables, cooked or pureed (4 tablespoons a day). Try spinach, beets, turnips, carrots, collard greens.
- Continue to feed your baby fruit, cooked, pureed, or raw (4 tablespoons a day).
- Continue to give your baby diluted fruit juice, which can now be diluted less or as tolerated (3 to 4 ounces per day).
- Introduce pureed meats, egg yolk, mashed beans (no skins), cottage cheese, or plain low-fat yogurt (4 tablespoons or more per day).
- Continue to use teething foods (hard dry toast, soda crackers without salt).
- If your baby has sufficient teeth and chewing skills, you may offer ground meats or poultry in lieu of pureed, or mild unprocessed cheese. Ground meat has more texture than pureed.

FEEDING BABIES TEN MONTHS OF AGE

When he is eight to ten months of age, your baby's dietary needs increase dramatically.

- Provide breast milk on demand (three to four feedings in twenty-four hours) or formula (usually a drinking cup), for a total of 24 to 32 ounces each day.
- Offer water as needed.
- Give vitamins and minerals only if prescribed by your doctor.
- Continue to feed cereal (4 tablespoons or more per day).
- Continue to feed vegetables, cooked, pureed, or raw (4 tablespoons or more per day). Hold off on introducing raw vegetables to your baby's diet. She does not have enough teeth yet to handle chewing stringy celery or crispy zucchini. However, you can offer soft-cooked vegetables in strips or slices.
- Continue to feed fruit, cooked, pureed, or raw (4 tablespoons or more per day). Babies can also have soft cooked fruits in pieces.
- Continue to offer non-diluted fruit juice as tolerated (4 to 8 ounces per day).
- Offer a choice of ground, strained, or pureed meats; egg yolk; strained soft-cooked beans; unprocessed cheese, cottage cheese, or low-fat plain yogurt (4 tablespoons or more per day).
- Continue to feed teething foods: hard, dry toast; soda crackers; bread sticks, as needed.
- Offer plain cooked (soft) pasta, such as macaroni, alphabet letters and numbers, pastini, or orzo (smaller pastas). As your baby accumulates more teeth, he will be able to handle the larger cooked pastas such as wheels, shells, and ziti.
- Begin offering small amounts of foods from the table (mashed potato, slices of soft peeled fruit).
- From ten months on, babies usually enjoy real finger foods. Give your baby bite-

size pieces of fresh peeled, pitted fruit; tofu chunks; or small pieces of soft meat and poultry.

FEEDING BABIES ELEVEN TO TWELVE MONTHS OF AGE

When she is eleven to twelve months of age, your baby's dietary needs continue to increase, and her tastebuds are developing.

- Provide breast milk (three or more feedings in twenty-four hours), formula, or cow's milk (8 ounces per serving) with your pediatrician's approval (three feedings in twenty-four hours using a cup or bottle).
- Continue to offer cereal (4 tablespoons or more per day).
- Continue to offer vegetables (4 tablespoons or more of bite-size pieces).
- Continue to offer fruit (4 tablespoons or more of bite-size pieces).
- Continue to offer undiluted fruit juice (8 ounces or more per day).
- Continue to offer water as needed.
- Offer ground or bite-size choices of meat, poultry, fish (be very careful to avoid fish with bones—try tuna!), unstrained cooked beans and lentils, cottage cheese, unprocessed mild cheese, or low-fat plain yogurt (4 to 6 tablespoons or more per day).
- Continue to offer teething foods.
- Offer a variety of regular table foods including mild casserole dishes. She may now be feeding herself.

At twelve months, your baby should be able to eat almost everything the family is eating. He should be drinking from a cup. You may now include whole eggs, diluted orange juice, and cow's milk in his diet. If he rejects a certain food or beverage, do not urge him to eat or drink it. He may need time to "learn to like" certain foods. Be patient. Simply try again.

Remember, toddlers have smaller appetites. Do not become overly concerned if your one-year-old suddenly stops eating as much as she used to. Your baby may have gained twelve to twenty pounds the first year of life, but will probably only gain six to eight pounds during the second year. Babies do more developing and less growing during this period. As growth rates slow after the first year, your baby's appetite usually declines.

At this point, your baby will be receiving most of her nutrition from solid foods. It is recommended that you increase the amount of protein in her diet. Tofu is an easy-to-use form of protein that is made from nutritious soybean and is found in most grocery stores. Beans work best when combined with grains to produce a more complete protein. For a young baby, make hummus, a combination of sesame paste (tahini) and ground chick-peas. If you like, you can puree meat and poultry from your table. Fish, similar to egg whites, tends to cause an allergic reaction in young children, so offer sparingly.

FOODS FOR BABIES WITH TEETH

As your baby grows, his teeth will develop, allowing the introduction of new food experiences. Some of these include:

- beef, cooked to at least 150°F, extra lean, finely chopped
- poultry, skinned, well-cooked, and finely chopped
- pasta
- egg yolk (before twelve months of age and then add whole egg at twelve months)
- avocado, raw and peeled
- cooked potatoes, sweet and white
- cooked broccoli
- cooked peas

- cooked cauliflower
- cooked and strained dried peas and beans, offer sparingly in case of gas
- cooked spinach
- cooked green beans
- pears, best fully ripened and raw
- cantaloupe and other melons (turns into a great slush when whirled with a bit of mango)

Combinations are a great way to introduce a new food that your baby may not presently enjoy. Try apple-banana, applesauce-squash, mango-pear, carrot-squash, and so on. Mixed flavors can help introduce a new food, or reawaken baby's taste for an old favorite. Carrots and peanut butter make a nice spread, and spinach pureed in a blender makes a tasty spaghetti topping. Other great mashed partners include sweet potato–avocado, carrot–white potato, and any combination of the above listed foods.

By now your baby can eat almost anything. She has teeth, so she can chew more, and her digestive system can handle whole milk, whole eggs, yogurt, fish, and wheat. Your baby may want to feed herself by now, and you should encourage this as much as possible. You will still have to cut up the food, but she can pick up the pieces with her hands and put them in her mouth. By this time, she should be eating at the table with the rest of the family.

RECOMMENDED DAILY SERVINGS

Offer several servings from each food group daily, at mealtimes or as snacks throughout the day. A complete dinner with the recommended servings for your one year old might include a cube of cheese or meat, ten peas, a few bites of boiled potato, 2 ounces of juice, and perhaps some fruit for dessert. Offering different-colored foods is a great incentive to get your baby to eat while also offering nutritional variety. Try to serve a green, yellow, orange, or red vegetable at both lunch and dinner. If you start your toddler on crisp, crunchy salads and vegetable snacks, he will develop a taste for fresh raw vegetables.

The United States Department of Agriculture's new food guide pyramid emphasizes foods from the five food groups. Each of these food groups provides some, but not all, of the nutrients we need. For good health, we need them all.

On the top of the pyramid are fats, oils, and sweets, which should be used sparingly. Two to three servings of milk, yogurt, and cheese should be offered each day, as well as meat, poultry, and fish. Your baby or toddler should get three to five servings of vegetables, and two to four servings of fruits. Bread, cereal, rice, and pasta make up the base of the pyramid, and six to eleven servings per day are recommended.

What is a serving? A slice of bread is one serving, and so is ¾ cup cereal. A bagel or muffin counts as two; a pasta dinner is usually three. But these are adult servings.

The following eating guide will give you a general idea of what your baby should be consuming during an average day.

SAMPLE EATING GUIDE FOR THE ONE- TO TWO-YEAR-OLD

Food Group	Daily Servings	Average Size of Servings
Milk	4	½ to 1 cup
Meat/protein	2 to 3	
Meat, fish, poultry		2 to 4 tablespoons
Dried peas and beans		2 to 4 tablespoons
Peanut butter		2 tablespoons
Eggs		1 egg
Cheese		1 to 2 ounces
Tofu/bean curd		2 to 4 tablespoons

Food Group	Daily Servings	Average Size of Servings
Fruits and vegetables	*4*	*2 to 4 tablespoons*
Breads and cereals	*4*	*½ slice bread;*
		¼ cup cereal
Whole grains (cooked rice)		*2 tablespoons*
Fat (oil, butter, margarine)	*3*	*1 teaspoon*
Dressing		*⅛ avocado*

Here are some suggestions for a well-balanced daily meal plan for baby:

Breakfast

- ¾ cup baby oatmeal and half a mashed banana mixed with formula or breast milk to the desired consistency (usually ½ cup)
- ¾ cup rice cereal and half of a pureed peach mixed with formula or breast milk
- ¾ cup cereal of choice and 2 ounces of any baby fruit juice (apple, pear) mixed with formula or breast milk
- 1 hard-cooked egg yolk (for babies ten months or older) mixed with approximately 1 ounce of formula or breast milk
- ¾ cup rice cereal and one-quarter of a pureed papaya mixed with formula or breast milk
- ¾ cup baby oatmeal and ¼ cup pureed applesauce mixed with formula or breast milk
- ¾ cup barley cereal and one-quarter of a pureed mango mixed with formula or breast milk
- ¾ cup brown rice cereal and two pureed prunes mixed with formula or breast milk

- At every breakfast, offer juice in a spouted cup (approximately 2 ounces or more)

Lunch
- 3 ounces of soft tofu, and one whole piece of fruit (Place in a food processor and puree until you have the desired consistency. You can also add two half pieces of fruit for variety: banana, peach; applesauce, mango.)
- ½ cup nonfat plain yogurt and ¾ cup cooked brown rice mixed with formula or breast milk to the desired consistency
- ¾ cup cooked pasta, pieces of unprocessed cheese, and formula or breast milk pureed in a food processor and served warm
- 2 ounces of juice or cow's milk (twelve months of age)

Snacks (Morning and Afternoon)
- teething biscuits, zwieback toast
- hard carrot
- plain bread sticks (ten months and older)
- ½ cup nonfat plain yogurt
- semi-stale sourdough bread (most babies love gumming the crust)
- bagels (large or mini), cut in half, toasted, or left whole overnight to get stale
- unsalted crackers (ten months and older)
- ½ cup unsweetened dry cereal (Cheerios, Kix)
- ½ banana cut up into small pieces (ten months and older)
- 2 ounces of juice

Dinner

You can add cereal to any vegetable/formula combination to make it a meal. Offer ½ cup pureed fruit at the end of the meal.

- ¼ cup pureed cooked carrots and ¾ cup cooked brown rice mixed with formula or milk to desired consistency
- ¼ cup pureed cooked broccoli and ¾ cup high-protein cereal mixed with formula or milk to desired consistency
- ¼ cup pureed cooked Swiss chard and ¾ cup cooked barley mixed with formula or milk to desired consistency
- ¼ cup cooked brown rice, 1 ounce pureed cooked turkey or chicken mixed with formula or milk to desired consistency
- ¼ cup pureed cooked sweet potatoes, 1 ounce pureed cooked chicken mixed with formula or milk to desired consistency
- ¼ cup mashed cooked potatoes, 1 ounce pureed cooked meat mixed with formula or milk to desired consistency
- ¼ cup pureed cooked beets, ¾ cup cooked brown rice mixed with formula or milk to desired consistency

These are just a few suggestions. The following chapters go into much more depth regarding recipes.

FEEDING HINTS

- For toddlers twelve months and older, offer small quantities of several different foods at each meal, because they tend to become disinterested in eating as their motor skills increase.
- Plan desserts as an integral nutritious part of the meal, not as a junk-food treat.

- Try to limit your toddler's intake of added sugar to 1 teaspoon a day.
- After twelve months, try to limit cow's milk to 16 ounces per day so your toddler doesn't fill up on milk.
- Offer small pieces of cut-up foods (one at a time) on the toddler's highchair tray, so he feels like he's participating in the feeding process.

2

The
Well Fed Baby
Breakfast

WE ALL KNOW HOW IMPORTANT A NOURISHING BREAK-
fast is. It sustains us through the morning hours until lunch. Your baby needs that nourishment too. But not everyone is ready to eat right after they wake up. If your baby refuses
food, try again later on, but don't let her wait until lunch before having the first food of the
day. Again, let your toddler experiment feeding herself. If your child enjoys breakfast, she
is more likely to eat it. Remember the amounts younger children eat will vary. A good
starting point for every meal is to offer 1 tablespoon of each food for each year of life.

Some of our recipes include milk, which you can substitute with formula or breast
milk if you so desire. For example, nursing mothers can add their breast milk to the baby's
cereal. For those babies who are allergic to milk-based formulas, use a soy-based formula
or Lactaid to replace milk. Please consult your pediatrician before using any of these.

All fresh fruits should be cooked until they are soft for babies up to eight months of
age. Bananas are the exception to the rule and can be used fresh. Fruits can be added to
cereals to give them a sweet taste. When your baby first starts on solids, just stick with

simple cereals that are iron fortified, then progress to farina and oatmeal. By the age of ten months, he should be able to tolerate all the recipes in this book with the recommended recipe modifications. Recipes that call for dried or fresh fruit should be cut small enough for his eating ability. Remember to cook all egg dishes well to kill any salmonella.

Breakfast can be as simple an offering as basic cooked grain. With so many varieties of grains on the market today, it is confusing to know how to prepare each one, so we have included a cooking guide to alleviate any confusion.

In all of our recipes, soy milk can be used in place of cow's milk; tofu can be used in place of meat; chicken should be free-range; and beef should be organically raised and hormone-free.

GRAIN COOKING GUIDE

Grain (1 cup uncooked)	Liquid (Cups)	Cooking Time (Minutes)	Yield (Cups)
Barley			
Regular pearl	3 to 4	50 to 60	4
Quick cooking	3	10 to 12	3
Quinoa	2	15	3
Quick-cooking oats	3	10 to 12	3
Rice			
Aromatic (white)	1¾	15	3 to 3½
Brown	2½	45 to 50	3 to 4
Brown, fast cooking	1¼	10 to 15	2
Long-grain	1¾ to 2	15	3
Medium (short-grain)	1½	15	3
Parboiled	2½	20 to 25	3 to 4
Precooked	1 (boiling)	Let stand 5 to 10	2

Grain (1 cup uncooked)	Liquid (Cups)	Cooking Time (Minutes)	Yield (Cups)
Rice (continued)			
Wild	2½ to 3	35 to 50	3 to 4
Wheat			
Bulgur	2	10	3
Couscous	1½	Let stand 5	2⅔
Cornmeal	4	20	3 to 4

PREPARING GRAINS

Ground Grains

Whole grains can be ground fresh on the day they are to be served. Grind the whole grain in a grinder, blender, food processor, or food mill. I would suggest a combination of wheat, oats, and rye. Equal amounts of each can be used, or, if preferred, more wheat and oats can be used in proportion to rye.

To cook, follow the amounts and directions above. Begin cooking the cereal about 45 minutes before serving time, because it takes this long for the non-quick-cooking grains.

Pressure-Cooked Wheat

Rinse the wheat and place it in a pressure cooker; cover with double the amount of water. Cook for 20 minutes at 10 pounds pressure. Drain and store the cooked wheat in the freezer for future use.

Crock-Pot Method

The evening before, place 1⅓ cups wheat, rye, barley, oats, or a combination, and 2⅔ cups warm water in a Crock-Pot. Turn it on low and let it cook all night. Makes three to four servings.

Breakfast Egg Yolk

Makes 1 serving

1 hard-boiled egg yolk
1 tablespoon formula or breast milk

✿

Puree the yolk with liquid formula until smooth. Serve lukewarm.

Recommended for ages 7 months+

Cooked Baby Fruits

MAKES 1 TO 2 SERVINGS

½ cup chopped cooked fruit
2 tablespoons cooking liquid from fruit, or use fruit juice (apple, pear, etc.)

❀

Place the fruit in a steamer and steam for about 5 minutes, until soft but not mushy.

Place the fruit and liquid in a food processor or blender and blend to the desired degree of smoothness.

Store in an airtight, clean container and refrigerate.

Recommended for ages 7 months+

Raw Baby Fruits

¾ cup chopped, peeled fruit
1 teaspoon fruit juice
1 teaspoon lemon juice water (1 quart water with 1 tablespoon lemon juice)

❁

Remove the skin and seeds from the fruit.

Place the fruit, juice, and lemon juice water in a food processor or blender and blend to the desired degree of smoothness. If the fruit does not liquefy easily, add another teaspoon of lemon juice water. This water helps prevent darkening of raw fruits. Store in a clean, airtight container and refrigerate.

Recommended for ages 8 months+. Infants tend to be able to tolerate ripe. raw fruit at this age.

Blueberry Yogurt Breakfast

½ cup ripe blueberries, washed, or frozen berries, thawed
1 cup plain nonfat yogurt
¼ cup cooked oatmeal

✿

Combine all the ingredients in a food processor or blender and process until smooth. Serve warm or at room temperature. Store leftovers in the refrigerator for no more than 2 days.

Recommended for ages 10 months+

Plums, Bananas, and Rice

MAKES 1 TO 2 SERVINGS

1 ripe plum, washed, skinned, and pitted
1 ripe banana
1 cup cooked brown rice (page 41)

❖

Combine all the ingredients in a food processor and blend until smooth. Serve warm or at room temperature.

Recommended for ages 7 months+

Peach Banana Oatmeal

MAKES 1 TO 2 SERVINGS

1 ripe peach, peeled, pitted, and cut up
1 cup cooked oatmeal
1 ripe banana

✿

Combine all the ingredients in a food processor and blend until smooth. Serve warm or at room temperature.

Recommended for ages 7 months+

Apple-Date Yogurt Breakfast

MAKES 2 SERVINGS

½ cup nonfat yogurt
¼ cup sliced ripe apples
½ cup cooked barley (page 41)
2 dates, ripe and pitted
Formula, for additional liquid

✿

Combine all the ingredients above except the formula in a food processor, and blend until smooth.

Add formula, 2 tablespoons at a time, if you require additional liquid.

Recommended for ages 8 months+

Warm Banana and Apple Compote with Cereal

Executive chef Hans Wiegand, Claremont Resort and Tennis Club

M A K E S   2   S E R V I N G S

1 apple, peeled and sliced
1 banana, peeled and sliced
2 bowls baby's favorite warm cereal

In a steamer, steam the apples until soft, about 5 minutes. Add the bananas to the steamer for about 1 minute.

Serve the apples and bananas either on top of baby's favorite cereal or on the side.

Recommended for ages 7 months+ (puree the mixture for infants who cannot tolerate texture)

Orange Puree

Chef-instructor John Jensen, California Culinary Academy

MAKES 4 SERVINGS

2 cups orange juice (fresh or concentrate)
1 teaspoon cornstarch
1 tablespoon water
¼ cup sugar

Place the orange juice in a saucepan over medium-high heat. Combine the cornstarch and water and mix thoroughly.

When the orange juice begins to simmer, add the cornstarch and water and stir. Lower the heat to medium and cook slowly, stirring constantly, until the mixture thickens and becomes somewhat glossy, 2 to 3 minutes.

Add the sugar and cook until the sugar dissolves and the mixture is smooth, another 2 to 3 minutes. Add to cottage cheese, yogurt, or cereal and serve cool.

Recommended for ages 10 months+

Cherry Tapioca

Chef-instructor John Jensen, California Culinary Academy

MAKES 3 SERVINGS

3 cups water
¼ cup infant cherry juice
¼ cup granulated tapioca
1 cup pitted fresh, canned, or frozen bing cherries, cut up
1 teaspoon sugar

In a saucepan, combine the water and juice. Bring to a boil, add the tapioca, and cook at a boil until the tapioca is translucent, about 5 minutes.

Remove from the heat and immediately add the cherries and sugar. Set aside to cool. May also be served warm.

Recommended for ages 8 months+

Bronwyn's Favorite Breakfast Cereal

Chef-instructor Mial Parker, California Culinary Academy

MAKES 2 SERVINGS

1 cup brown rice
2 tablespoons sesame seeds
¼ cup adzuki beans (available in any grocery or health food store)
¼ cup millet
3 cups water
Maple syrup, brown rice syrup, or strained fruit to taste (optional)

❀

Preheat the oven to 325°F. Place the rice, sesame seeds, beans, and millet on a cookie sheet and toast them until they're golden brown, turning occasionally, about 5 minutes. Remove from the oven and allow them to cool slightly.

Place the toasted grains in a food processor or grinder and grind them to a fine meal. The meal may be stored at this point in a refrigerator for up to 1 month.

To prepare the cereal, in a saucepan, bring the water to a boil, add the cereal, reduce the heat to medium-low, and simmer, stirring occasionally, until the meal is tender, about 30 minutes.

Serve warm with maple syrup or brown rice syrup, if desired. Strained fruit may also be added.

Recommended for ages 6 months+

Brown Rice Cereal

Executive chef Amy Ferguson-Ota, Ritz Carlton Mauna Lani

MAKES 4 SERVINGS

1 cup brown rice
1½ cups water
2 cups milk
Pureed fruit to taste

Mix all the ingredients together in a saucepan over medium-low heat. Cook uncovered until the rice is creamy in texture about 20 to 25 minutes.

Add the pureed fruit and serve.

Recommended for ages 6 months+

Fruity Farina

3 cups milk
½ cup farina (Cream of Wheat or couscous)
5 tablespoons apple juice
1 teaspoon ground cinnamon

❧

Heat the milk in a saucepan over medium heat. When warm, add the farina by sprinkling it on top of the milk. Cook, stirring constantly, until thickened, about 5 minutes. Remove from the heat.

Stir in the apple juice and cinnamon and serve.

Recommended for ages 8 months+

Banana and Barley

MAKES 1 SERVING

¼ cup quick-cooking pearl barley
1¼ cups milk
½ banana, peeled and mashed

Place the barley and milk in a saucepan and cook over medium heat until the barley is tender, 20 to 25 minutes. Taste the barley to make sure it is done and not too crunchy.

Add the mashed banana, stir, and cook for 30 seconds. Remove from the heat immediately and serve warm.

Recommended for ages 6 months+

Breakfast Rice

½ cup rice
1 cup milk
¾ cup water
¼ fresh banana, peeled and mashed

Combine the rice, milk and ½ cup of the water in a saucepan, cover, and cook over medium heat until the liquid has been absorbed, 20 to 25 minutes.

Remove from the heat, uncover, and allow to cool to room temperature. Cover and let sit in the refrigerator overnight to let the starch set up.

Remove the rice from the refrigerator. Stir in the remaining ¼ cup of water, cover, and cook over medium heat for 10 minutes, stirring occasionally.

Add the bananas and stir. Cook a few more minutes and serve warm.

Recommended for ages 6 months+

Millet and Peaches

1 cup millet
4 cups water
¼ cup pureed peaches

Place the millet and water in the top of a double boiler, bring the water in the bottom pot to a boil, and cook on high heat for 5 minutes. (The millet will scorch over direct heat, which makes a double boiler necessary.)

Reduce the heat to medium-low and let the millet simmer for 30 to 45 minutes, until it is tender. Turn off the heat and let it stand for a few minutes.

Stir in the pureed peaches and serve.

Recommended for ages 6 months+

Chunky Pear-Applesauce

3 ripe apples, peeled, cored, and chopped into ¼-inch pieces
3 ripe pears, peeled, cored, and quartered
½ cup water
1 tablespoon lemon juice
¼ cup frozen apple juice concentrate, thawed
¼ teaspoon ground cinnamon
½ cup uncooked cereal (oatmeal, rice, or barley)
¼ cup formula

Place the first six ingredients in a heavy saucepan. Bring to a boil over medium heat, then reduce the heat to medium-low. Cover and cook, stirring occasionally, until the mixture is reduced to a soft sauce, about 10 minutes.

Remove from the heat, bring to room temperature, or refrigerate until needed.

When ready to use, mix ¼ cup of this mixture with ½ cup cooked cereal, along with 2 tablespoons of formula at a time, until you have the desired consistency.

Recommended for ages 7 months+

Plums and Yogurt

MAKES 2 SERVINGS

2 ripe plums, peeled and pitted
½ cup nonfat plain yogurt

Combine the plums and yogurt and puree in a food processor until they're smooth. Serve at room temperature or chilled. (Any ripe fruit can be used in place of plums, but avoid strawberries until your baby is 12 months of age.) Cooked cereal may be added to give this yogurt more texture.

Recommended for ages 8 months+

Fruit Compote

¼ *fresh peach, peeled and pitted*
¼ *fresh pear, peeled and cored*
4 slices banana
2 tablespoons apple juice

Place all the ingredients into a saucepan over medium-high heat and cook, uncovered, until the fruit is tender, 10 to 15 minutes.

Remove from the heat. Puree in a blender, and serve. (You may want to allow the fruit to cool slightly before pureeing to avoid possible burns.)

Canned fruit may be substituted for fresh (use fruit canned in its own juices rather than sugar). If you use canned fruit, there is no need to cook the fruit, just puree it and serve.

Recommended for ages 7 months+

Frittata

1½ teaspoons safflower oil
4 large egg yolks
¼ cup vegetable puree (any vegetable pureed in a blender)

Preheat the oven to 325°F. Brush a 6-inch ovenproof skillet or pan with oil.

Whisk the egg yolks and vegetable puree together. Pour into the skillet, place in the oven, and bake until the eggs are firm, about 45 minutes.

Remove the skillet from the oven and let cool slightly. Cut the frittata into bite-size pieces.

Recommended for ages 10 months+

Chunky Fruit

1 ripe banana
2 cups blueberries, rinsed and picked over
1 cup peeled and chopped peaches
½ cup unsweetened applesauce
1 tablespoon frozen apple juice concentrate, thawed

❁

Place all of the ingredients in a food processor and puree or chop. Serve warm or chilled.

Recommended for ages 8 months+

Cottage Cheese Fruit

½ cup cottage cheese
½ cup ½-inch slices peeled ripe banana, mango, and/or apricot
4 to 6 tablespoons apple juice (orange juice for 12 months+)

✿

Combine all the ingredients in a food processor and puree until the mixture is of the desired consistency. Serve cool.

Recommended for ages 8 months+

Tropical Treat

½ ripe avocado, peeled and pitted
½ ripe banana, peeled
¼ cup cottage cheese or low-fat plain yogurt

Combine all the ingredients and puree them until they reach the desired consistency. Serve at room temperature or cool. This mixture may be added to any cereal of choice.

Recommended for ages 8 months+

The Well Fed Baby Breakfast

3

*

The
Well Fed Baby
Breads

THE USDA'S NEW FOOD GUIDE PYRAMID SUGGESTS that bread, cereal, rice, and pasta should be the basics of our diet. It is also recommended that we have six to eleven servings from this group per day. The following bread, muffin, biscuit, and polenta recipes are some of the tastiest we have ever found, and have adult-size servings.

In all of our recipes, soy milk can be used in place of cow's milk; tofu can be used in place of meat; chicken should be free-range; and beef should be organically raised and hormone-free.

Blueberry Breakfast Popovers

Executive chef and co-owner Bert Cutino, Sardine Factory, Monterey, California

MAKES 10 TO 12 POPOVERS

1⅓ cups all-purpose flour
2 teaspoons sugar
1 cup milk
1 large egg plus 1½ large egg whites
1 cup fresh blueberries
Vegetable spray or fine coating with margarine

❀

Preheat the oven to 450°F.

Combine the flour and sugar and set aside.

Combine the milk, egg, and egg whites in a bowl and whisk until they're blended. Gradually add the flour mixture and stir until it's homogeneous. Don't overstir the mixture or it won't rise properly. Add the blueberries.

Place the popover pan in the oven for 3 minutes. Remove and coat with cooking spray or margarine.

Divide the popover mixture into the cups and bake for 10 minutes. Reduce the heat to 350°F and bake until the popovers are golden brown, about 25 minutes.

Remove from the pan and serve immediately. Cut into bite-size pieces.

Recommended for ages 10 months+

The Well Fed Baby Breads

Oatmeal Shortbread Biscuits

Executive chef Phyllis Bologna. National Accounts Development.
General Foods USA Foodservice Division

MAKES 12 BISCUITS

1 cup all-purpose unbleached flour
1 tablespoon sugar
1 teaspoon baking powder
½ teaspoon salt
2 cups quick-cooking rolled (old-fashioned) oats
½ cup (1 stick) unsalted butter, softened and cut into small pieces
½ cup milk

Preheat the oven to 375°F. Grease a cookie sheet.

Sift together the flour, sugar, baking powder, and salt into a mixing bowl. Add the oats, then cut in the butter using a pastry cutter or 2 knives until the mixture is crumbly.

Gradually add the milk, stirring until a dough is formed. Roll the dough to ⅛-inch thickness, or, if you have an eager pair of small hands available, let them pat out the dough. Cut into irregular squares.

Bake the biscuits on the cookie sheet until they're lightly browned, 12 to 15 minutes. Serve at room temperature with apple butter or strawberry jam. Cut into bite-size pieces.

Recommended for ages 10 months+

Basic Polenta

Chef-owner Lidia Bastianich. Felidia's Ristorante (Reprinted by permission from La Cucina di Lidia.)

MAKES 4 SERVINGS

4 cups water
1 tablespoon unsalted butter
1 bay leaf
2 tablespoons coarse salt
1½ cups coarse yellow cornmeal

In a medium-size cast-iron saucepan or other heavy pot, bring all the ingredients except the cornmeal to simmer over medium heat.

Very slowly, begin to sift cornmeal into the pan through the fingers of one hand, stirring constantly with a wooden spoon or whisk. Gradually sift the remaining meal into the pan, continue to stir, and reduce the heat to medium-low. Stir until the polenta is smooth and thick and pulls away from the sides of the pan as it is stirred, about 30 minutes.

Discard the bay leaf, pour the polenta into a serving bowl or onto a wooden board, and allow it to rest for 10 minutes. To serve from the bowl, dip a large spoon into water and scoop the polenta onto individual dishes, dipping the spoon into the water between scoops. To serve from the board, cut polenta into segments with a thin, taut string or knife and transfer to plates with a spatula or cake knife.

Recommended for ages 10 months+

Chef Rachel's Bagels

MAKES 12 BAGELS

2 packages active dry yeast
4¼ to 4½ cups sifted all-purpose unbleached flour
1½ cups lukewarm water
¼ cup sugar
1 tablespoon salt

✿

In a large mixing bowl, combine the yeast and 1¾ cups of the flour.

Combine the water, 3 tablespoons of the sugar, and the salt. Add to the yeast mixture. Beat at low speed with an electric mixer for 30 seconds, scraping the sides constantly. Beat for 3 minutes at high speed.

By hand, stir in enough of the remaining flour to make a moderately stiff dough. Turn out onto a lightly floured board and knead until the dough is smooth, 5 to 8 minutes. Cover with a clean kitchen cloth and let rise for 20 minutes.

In a large kettle, combine a gallon of water and the remaining tablespoon of sugar; bring to a boil. Reduce the heat to medium, simmering.

Preheat the oven to 375°F.

Take about one handful of dough and roll it with the palms of your hands into a long tube about 1 inch thick, and attach each end of the tube to make a circle (looks like a doughnut).

Place 4 to 5 bagels, one at a time, into the water and allow them to simmer for 7 minutes, turning each bagel once. Remove the bagels from the water, shake off excess water and place them on an ungreased baking sheet.

Bake for 30 to 35 minutes. They should look golden brown when done.

Recommended for ages 8 months+. Initially, offer bagels frozen or stale for teething purposes.

Sturdy Teething Biscuits

MAKES 24 BISCUITS

1 tablespoon uncooked oatmeal
1 cup all-purpose unbleached flour
1 tablespoon soy flour (may be purchased at any health food store)
1 tablespoon wheat germ
1 tablespoon dry milk
1 large egg yolk, beaten
3 tablespoons honey
1 teaspoon pure vanilla extract
¼ cup milk
1½ tablespoons canola oil

❀

Preheat the oven to 350°F.

In a mixing bowl, blend the dry ingredients. Blend in the egg yolk, honey, vanilla, liquid milk, and oil. The dough should be stiff.

Roll the dough out thinly, about ¼ inch in thickness, on a floured surface and cut the dough into finger-length rectangles or desired shapes.

Bake on an ungreased cookie sheet for 15 minutes, until lightly browned. Cool and store in an airtight container.

Recommended for ages 8 months+. Please, never leave infants unattended when they are eating. Occasionally, they are able to bite off chunks that they can easily choke on.

Graham Crackers

1 cup graham or whole wheat flour
1 cup all-purpose unbleached flour
1 teaspoon baking powder
¼ cup (½ stick) margarine, softened
½ cup honey
¼ cup milk

✿

Preheat the oven to 400°F.

In a bowl, combine the flours and baking powder. Add the margarine, honey, and milk. Blend well.

Roll out the dough to ½-inch thickness and cut into squares. Prick them with a fork, then brush with the milk.

Bake on an ungreased baking sheet until golden brown, about 18 minutes. If rolled thicker, these crackers can be used as teething biscuits.

Recommended for ages 10 months+

Banana Bread Sticks

MAKES 2 DOZEN BREAD STICKS

1¾ cups all-purpose unbleached flour
2 teaspoons baking powder
½ teaspoon baking soda
¼ cup firmly packed brown sugar
½ cup canola oil
2 large eggs
1 cup mashed banana

Preheat the oven to 350°F. Grease a loaf pan.

In a bowl, combine the flour, baking powder, and baking soda. In a separate mixing bowl, cream together the sugar, oil, and eggs, then add the mashed banana, slowly mixing in the dry ingredients as you combine them. Do not beat or overmix.

Pour the mixture into the loaf pan and bake until a wooden skewer inserted into the loaf comes out clean, about 1 hour. Cool in the pan for about 15 minutes, then remove from the pan and cool for an additional 20 minutes on a wire rack.

Preheat the oven to 150°F. Slice the loaf into ⅜-inch slices, then cut each slice into four ½-inch-wide sticks. Spread the sticks out on an ungreased cookie sheet and bake until the sticks are crunchy, about 1 hour. Store in an airtight container for up to a week.

Recommended for ages 10 months+

Crumpets

MAKES 24 CRUMPETS

3 cups all-purpose unbleached flour
1 tablespoon baking powder
2 tablespoons sugar or honey
2 tablespoons margarine
1 large egg
1½ to 1¾ cups milk

❀

In a bowl, combine the flour, baking powder, and sugar or honey. Cut the margarine into the flour mixture using a pastry blender or 2 knives until the mixture has the consistency of bread crumbs.

In another bowl, beat the egg with the milk, then combine the dry ingredients into the wet ingredients and stir just enough to moisten.

Grease a griddle or pan and heat over medium heat. Drop 3 tablespoons batter per crumpet into a ring mold (see note) that is placed in the griddle or pan. Cook over medium heat until bubbles appear on top of the batter. Then remove the ring, turn the crumpet over, and cook until done. Crumpets are batter-colored and have lots of holes throughout them when they are done. Offer them toasted and cut into bite-size pieces.

Note: Because crumpet batter is so thin, you will need special 4- by 1-inch rings to make them. These are usually stainless steel and are available in most market places, packaged in sets of four. As a creative option, you may use clean non-lead tuna-fish cans, with the tops and bottoms removed.

Recommended for ages 10 months+

Pumpkin Muffins

1½ cups all-purpose unbleached flour
½ cup sugar
2 teaspoons baking powder
1 teaspoon ground cinnamon
½ teaspoon ground ginger
¼ teaspoon ground cloves
1 large egg, lightly beaten
½ cup milk
½ cup canned solid pack pumpkin
¼ cup (½ stick) margarine, melted
Topping: 2½ teaspoons sugar mixed with ½ teaspoon ground cinnamon

❁

Preheat the oven to 400°F. Lightly grease a large-size muffin tin.

Sift together the first 6 ingredients into a mixing bowl.

In a separate bowl, combine the egg, milk, pumpkin, and melted butter.

Add the wet ingredients to the sifted mixture, mixing only until combined. Fill the greased muffin cups two thirds full; sprinkle with the cinnamon sugar topping.

Bake for 20 to 25 minutes, until golden brown. Cut into bite-size pieces.

Recommended for ages 10 months+

Apple-Orange Muffins

MAKES 12 LARGE MUFFINS

1 cup whole-wheat flour
1 cup all-purpose unbleached flour
2 teaspoons baking soda
1¼ teaspoons baking powder
¼ cup dry milk
¼ cup frozen apple juice concentrate, thawed
¼ cup frozen orange juice concentrate, thawed
Juice of 2 oranges (this is okay for infants because it is such a small amount)
½ cup water
2 large eggs

Preheat the oven to 350°F. Grease a muffin tin.

In a mixing bowl, blend the dry ingredients together.

Stir in the juice concentrates, orange juice, and water. Add the eggs and blend until smooth.

Pour the batter into the cups, filling each about two thirds full. Bake until the muffins pull away from the sides of the pan or spring back when slightly pressed, 12 to 15 minutes. Cut into bite-size pieces.

Recommended for ages 10 months+

4

✿

The
Well Fed Baby
Lunch

MOST PARENTS NOTICE THAT THEIR CHILDREN TEND to eat more at lunch than at dinnertime, so it is very important to offer a well-balanced luncheon menu. Try to offer one item per food group, and don't be upset if your baby only tries a little from each. This is perfectly normal. Cheese tends to be a big favorite at lunchtime, and we encourage parents to offer natural cheese as opposed to processed. Read the ingredients on both packages, and we think you will agree that natural is better. According to the American Academy of Pediatrics (AAP), properly strained home-made foods are nutritionally equivalent if not superior to commercially prepared foods. Carrot juice can be used to replace sugar. For variety, flavor, and fun, beet juice and carrot juice can be added to mashed potatoes to make rainbow potatoes. We have found that pureed green beans and peas mix better when added to a combination of cereal and formula. By mixing them with just the formula, the texture is too chunky for a new eater. The following recipes are in infant proportions.

In all of our recipes, soy milk can be used in place of cow's milk; tofu can be used in place of meat; chicken should be free-range; and beef should be organically raised and hormone-free.

Legumes (Beans, Peas, Lentils)

MAKES 2 1/2 CUPS

1 cup any dried legume
3 cups water
¾ cup milk

✿

Rinse the legumes. Soak in water and cover overnight, or you can bring them to a boil for 2 minutes, cover, and allow them to set for 2 hours.

Drain the legumes, then combine with the water in a saucepan, bring to a boil, then reduce the heat to medium-low and simmer until tender. For example: Lima beans will take 1 hour, black-eyed peas 30 minutes.

When the legumes are soft, remove them from the heat, drain off all the remaining water and, if you prefer, puree them with a food mill or blender, or mash with a fork. Add the milk to thin. Press through a sieve to remove any pulp. Place the legumes in small containers or in a divided ice cube tray and freeze until needed. One serving would be about 2 tablespoons.

Recommended for ages 7 months+

Baby Vegetables (Cooked)

½ cup cut-up cooked vegetables (page 87)
2 tablespoons formula or cooking liquid from vegetables

❀

Place the vegetables and liquid in a food mill, blender, or food processor and process to the desired degree of smoothness.

Store in a clean, airtight container in the refrigerator.

Recommended for ages 7 months+

Cooked Vegetables

❁

A variety of vegetables can be prepared. Some good choices are green beans, peas, squash, carrots, spinach, or sweet potatoes.

How to prepare vegetables: Wash the vegetable, cut off the covering if necessary, and cut into ½-inch pieces. Add ¼ cup boiling water for 1 cup vegetables. Steam over medium-low heat until they're tender, about 5 minutes. Blend or puree until smooth, if desired. Add the cooking liquid or formula for additional liquid. Let cool, and use immediately, or freeze.

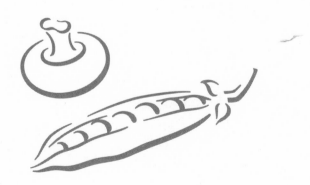

Peas and Brown Rice

1 cup frozen or fresh peas, cooked in water to cover until tender
1 cup cooked brown rice (page 41)
½ cup formula

✿

Combine the peas, rice, and ¼ cup of the formula in a food processor, blender, or food mill and blend until smooth. If the consistency is too thick, add more formula, 2 tablespoons at a time, until the rice reaches the desired consistency.

Serve warm or at room temperature. Store leftovers in the refrigerator for no more than 2 days.

Recommended for ages 7 months+

Corn and Butternut Squash

MAKES 1 TO 2 SERVINGS

1 cup water
½ ear corn, or ½ cup frozen corn
½ cup peeled bite-size pieces butternut squash
¼ cup formula

❁

Put the water in a saucepan with a steamer basket and bring to a boil. Add the corn to the steamer basket, steam for 7 minutes, and cut kernels from the husk. If using frozen corn, steam for 2 to 3 minutes, until the kernels are tender.

Steam the squash until it's soft, 5 to 8 minutes.

Combine the corn and squash and half of the formula in a food processor, food mill, or blender and process until the vegetables are smooth. Add more formula until you reach the desired consistency.

Serve warm or at room temperature.

Note: You can add 3 ounces of pureed soft tofu to make a complete lunch.

Recommended for ages 7 months+

Apples, Plums, and Blueberries

MAKES 1 TO 2 SERVINGS

1 cup water
1 apple, peeled, cored, and sliced
1 ripe plum, peeled and pitted
¼ cup ripe blueberries, picked over, or frozen, use thawed

Put the water in a saucepan with a steamer basket and bring to a boil. Place the apple slices in the steamer basket and steam until tender, about 5 minutes.

Combine the apple, plum, and blueberries in a food processor, food mill, or blender and process until they're smooth. Serve at room temperature or chilled.

Note: You can add 3 ounces of pureed soft tofu or ¼ cup cottage cheese, pureed, to make a complete lunch.

Recommended for ages 7 months+

Apples and Apricots

MAKES 1 SERVING

1 cup water
1 apple, peeled, cored, and sliced
1 ripe apricot, peeled and pitted

❁

Put the water in a saucepan with a steamer basket and bring to a boil. Put the sliced apple and apricot in the steamer basket and steam until tender, about 5 minutes.

Combine the apple and apricot in a food processor, food mill, or blender and process until they're smooth. Serve at room temperature or chilled.

Note: You can add 3 ounces of pureed soft tofu or ¼ cup cottage cheese, pureed, to make a complete lunch.

Recommended for ages 7 months+

Peaches and Mango

MAKES 1 TO 2 SERVINGS

1 ripe peach, peeled, pitted, and cut up
1 ripe mango, peeled, pitted, and cut up (papaya may be substituted for mango)

❀

Combine the peach and mango in a food processor, food mill, or blender and puree until they're smooth. Serve at room temperature or chilled.

Note: You can add 3 ounces of pureed soft tofu or ¼ cup cottage cheese, pureed, to make a complete lunch.

Recommended for ages 7 months+

Pears and Raspberrries

MAKES 2 SERVINGS

2 ripe pears, peeled and cored
1 cup ripe raspberries, gently rinsed and patted dry

Combine the ingredients in a food processor, food mill, or blender and process until they're smooth. Serve warm, at room temperature, or chilled.

Note: Add 3 ounces of pureed soft tofu or ¼ cup cottage cheese, pureed, to make a complete lunch.

Recommended for ages 10 months+

Rice Congee

Chef Martin Yan, Yan Can Cook

MAKES 6 TO 8 SERVINGS

1¼ cups uncooked long-grain rice
4 thin slices fresh peeled ginger
12 cups chicken broth
½ pound boneless, skinless chicken breast, or firm tofu, julienned

Combine the rice, ginger, and broth in a large pot and bring to a boil. Cover, reduce the heat to medium-low, and simmer, stirring occasionally, until the rice becomes very soft and creamy, about 1½ hours.

Remove the ginger slices. Add the chicken or tofu and simmer for 8 minutes more, stirring occasionally. Puree or chop in a food processor if your baby cannot handle the thick consistency. Serve warm or at room temperature.

Recommended for ages 10 months+

Carrot Puree with Mint

Chef Kenneth C. Wolfe, Wolfe's Cooking School

MAKES 2 SERVINGS

2 tablespoons butter
¾ pound young carrots, scrubbed and thinly sliced
1 teaspoon sugar
Several fresh mint leaves

❧

Melt the butter in a skillet, then add the carrots, sugar, mint leaves, and a few drops of water. Cover tightly, and stew over low heat until the carrots are tender, about 15 minutes.

Remove the mint leaves, then place the carrots and their juice into a food processor or blender and pulse quickly into a fine puree. Or you can mash them with a fork for older infants. Check for taste and keep warm until serving.

Recommended for ages 7 months+

Bibby's Red Beans and Ham

Executive chef Suzette Gresham-Tognetti, Ristorante Acquerello

MAKES 4 SERVINGS

1 pound red beans
½ pound cooked ham, diced
7 cups cold water
1 bay leaf
1 small onion, diced
1 clove garlic
1 tablespoon sugar

Put all the ingredients together in a pot. Bring to a boil, then turn off the heat and allow the mixture to sit for 1 hour—the beans will plump.

Turn the heat to medium and gently simmer until the beans are tender, about 30 minutes. Remove the bay leaf and puree the mixture in a food processor. Serve warm or at room temperature.

Recommended for ages 8 months+

Tropical Fruit Salad

MAKES 2 SERVINGS

1 avocado, skinned and pitted
1 papaya, skinned
2 apples, skinned and cored
2 bananas, peeled
1 star fruit (carambola)
4 blueberries, cleaned and stems removed
3 ounces soft tofu, pureed (optional)

Slice the fruit, then puree together in a blender, food processor, or food mill. You can add the tofu to the mixture to make a complete lunch for baby. Serve cool or at room temperature.

Recommended for ages 7 months+

Naturally Fresh Applesauce

MAKES 1 PINT

8 medium apples, cored

❀

Preheat the oven to 350°F.

Wash and core the apples. Place the apples in a tightly covered baking dish with ½ inch of water. Bake until the apples are tender, 30 minutes for the softer varieties, 45 minutes for harder apples.

Strain through a sieve to remove the skin. Use a blender or processor to puree the apple pulp.

You can store the applesauce for up to one week in the refrigerator or freeze in ice cube trays.

Note: Add 3 ounces of pureed soft tofu or ¼ cup cottage cheese, pureed, to ¼ cup of the applesauce for a complete lunch.

Recommended for ages 7 months+

Beets and Barley

1 cup water, plus 1 tablespoon
3 medium beets, peeled, roots trimmed, and sliced
¼ cup cooked barley (page 41)

❁

Pour the cup of water into a saucepan with a steamer basket and bring to a boil.

Place the sliced beets in the steamer basket, cover, and steam until tender, about 10 minutes.

Place the beets in a blender, add the tablespoon of water, and puree. Add more water, if needed, until you have the desired consistency.

Add the cooked barley to the beets for a complete lunch. Serve warm or at room temperature.

Recommended for ages 7 months+

ℬaby Carrots and Brown Rice

MAKES 1 ½ CUPS

1 cup water
3 to 4 large carrots, scrubbed and sliced ½ inch thick
About ¼ cup formula or water
¼ cup cooked brown rice (page 41) or 3 ounces soft tofu

❁

Bring the water to a boil in a saucepan fitted with a steamer basket.

Add the carrots to the steamer, cover, and cook until tender, about 10 minutes.

Place the carrots in a blender or food processor, add the formula, and puree. Add more water or formula until you have the desired consistency. Add brown rice or tofu to make a complete meal.

Recommended for ages 7 months+

Chick-pea Puree and Barley

MAKES 1 TO 1 1/2 CUPS

2 cups cooked chick-peas
3 tablespoons formula
1/4 cup cooked barley (page 41)

❁

Place the ingredients in a food processor, blender, or food mill and process until smooth. Add more formula to achieve the consistency your baby can tolerate.

Recommended for ages 8 months+

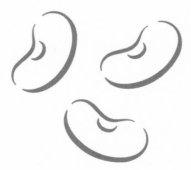

ʃtewed Dried Apricots and Tofu

MAKES 2 SERVINGS

1 cup dried apricots
1½ cups water
3 ounces soft tofu

❀

Soak the apricots in the water for 1 hour. In a saucepan, bring the apricots and water to a boil. Cover and simmer over medium-low heat until the apricots are tender, 15 to 25 minutes.

Let them cool. Add the tofu, place in a blender or food processor, and puree.

Recommended for ages 7 months+

Eggplant and Couscous

MAKES 4 SERVINGS

1 cup water
1 medium-size eggplant, peeled and cut into ½-inch pieces
1 cup cooked couscous (page 42)
2 tablespoons formula (optional)

Put the water in a saucepan with a steamer basket and bring to a boil. Add the eggplant to the steamer basket and steam until tender, 10 to 15 minutes. Or bake the eggplant in a preheated 325°F. oven for 15 to 25 minutes.

Puree the eggplant in a food processor, food mill, or blender.

Add the couscous and puree again. You may need to add the formula to make a smooth consistency. Serve warm or at room temperature.

Recommended for ages 7 months+

Baked Acorn Squash and Brown Rice

MAKES 2 SERVINGS

1 acorn or butternut squash
½ cup cooked brown rice (page 41)
2 tablespoons butter
½ cup formula

Preheat the oven to 350°F.

Scrub the squash, cut it in half, and scoop out the seeds. Place skin side up in an ovenproof dish containing 1 inch of water. Bake in the oven for 45 minutes. You can also cook the squash on the high setting in a microwave for 20 minutes.

Remove the flesh from the shells and place in a food processor, food mill, or blender. Add the rice, butter, and 2 tablespoons of the formula and puree until the mixture is smooth. Add additional formula, 1 tablespoon at a time, until you achieve the desired consistency. Serve warm or at room temperature.

Recommended for ages 7 months+

Carrot Apple Puree

MAKES 2 SERVINGS

1 cup water
1 carrot, scrubbed and sliced
1 apple, peeled, cored, and sliced
2 tablespoons formula
½ teaspoon butter
3 ounces soft tofu

Put the water in a saucepan with a steamer basket and bring to a boil. Add the carrot slices to the steamer basket and steam for 5 minutes. Then add the apple slices and steam until they're tender, about 5 minutes more.

Place all the ingredients in a food processor, food mill, or blender and puree until smooth. Serve warm or at room temperature.

Recommended for ages 7 months+

Carrots and Beets with Apple

MAKES 2 SERVINGS

2 medium-size carrots, scrubbed and thinly sliced
2 small beets, cooked in water to cover until tender, and diced
½ apple, peeled, cored, and diced
⅓ cup unsweetened apple juice

✿

Simmer the carrots, beets, and apple in a saucepan over medium-low heat in the apple juice until tender, about 10 minutes.

Puree in a food processor, food mill, or blender and serve warm or at room temperature.

Note: Add ½ cup of any cooked grain, if desired.

Recommended for ages 7 months+

$\int$weet Potato and Apple Puree

MAKES 2 SERVINGS

1 cup water
1 small sweet potato or yam, peeled and sliced
½ apple, peeled, cored, and sliced
2 tablespoons formula
½ teaspoon butter

Put the water in a saucepan with a steamer basket and bring to a boil. Add the sweet potato to the steamer basket and steam for 5 minutes. Add the apple slices and steam for an additional 5 minutes, or until they're tender.

Place all the ingredients in a food processor, food mill, or blender and process until they're smooth. You may need to add more formula for a more liquid consistency.

Recommended for ages 7 months+

Refried Beans

2 tablespoons olive oil
½ pound dried pinto beans, cooked according to package instructions,
drained but cooking liquid reserved; or one 15-ounce can plain pinto beans,
drained but liquid reserved

❀

Heat the oil over medium heat in a heavy skillet, then add the beans. As the beans simmer, mash them with a potato masher and stir. Add the reserved liquid several tablespoons at a time, to achieve the desired consistency. Simmer for about 20 minutes, stirring occasionally.

Transfer the beans to a food processor, food mill, or blender and puree. Strain through a sieve to remove the bean skins. Serve warm or at room temperature.

Note: You may add ½ cup cooked grain and formula to make a complete protein meal.

Recommended for ages 7 months+

Mango Puree

1 ripe mango, peeled, pitted, and cut into pieces
3 ounces soft tofu, or ½ cup cottage cheese

❖

Combine the mango and tofu or cottage cheese in a food processor, food mill, or blender, and puree. Serve cool or at room temperature.

Recommended for ages 7 months+

The Well Fed Baby Lunch

California Chicken

MAKES 4 SERVINGS

1 whole large skinless, boneless chicken breast, cooked and shredded
½ cup refried beans (page 108)
½ large avocado, peeled, pitted, and sliced
½ large tomato, peeled and chopped
2 tablespoons shredded Monterey jack cheese
½ cup nonfat plain yogurt

❖

Mix all the ingredients in a bowl and puree in a food processor, blender, or food mill. Serve cool or at room temperature. Refrigerate the leftovers and serve within 24 hours.

Recommended for ages 8 months+

Steamed Veggies

1 cup water
½ cup shredded carrots
½ cup shredded beets
½ cup shredded turnips
½ cup red pepper strips

Put the water in a saucepan with a steamer basket and bring to a boil. Add the vegetables to the steamer basket and steam until tender, about 8 minutes. Reserve the steaming water.

Transfer the vegetables to a blender, food processor, or food mill and puree. Use the liquid from steaming to achieve a smooth consistency.

Recommended for ages 7 months+

Vegetarian Chili Beans

MAKES 4 SERVINGS

2 cups dried kidney beans
3½ cups water
1 cup chopped onion
1 cup chopped celery
2½ cups peeled, seeded, and chopped fresh or canned tomatoes
1 clove garlic, peeled
½ cup cooked brown rice (page 41)

Soak the beans in 3 cups of the water overnight.

Preheat the oven to 250°F. Drain the beans, transfer to a casserole, and bake them until they're tender, about 3½ hours.

Combine the remaining ½ cup of water, the onion, and celery in a saucepan and cook over medium heat until they're tender, about 20 minutes. Add them to the beans.

Add the tomatoes and garlic to the beans and simmer over low heat for 30 minutes. Puree the beans in a food processor, blender, or food mill. Add the cooked brown rice and puree again. Serve warm or at room temperature.

Recommended for ages 10 months+

Black Beans and Rice

1 pound black beans
6 cups cold water
1 large onion, chopped
½ clove garlic, minced
1 pound brown rice, cooked (page 41)

❁

In a saucepan, combine the beans with the water, bring to a boil, and simmer over medium-high heat for 1 hour.

In a skillet, cook the onions and garlic in a little water until they're tender, 10 to 15 minutes. Add the onions and garlic to the beans and cook until the beans are tender and the liquid is thick, about 30 minutes.

Add the beans to the cooked brown rice and puree. Serve warm or at room temperature.

Recommended for ages 8 months+

5

❀

The
Well Fed Baby
Dinner

Dinnertime is usually a difficult time for most children and parents. Everyone is tired, and no one really feels like eating. However, we like to have our children at the dinner table with us in the evenings, which is not an easy feat. The pace at which we eat is rather rapid, as it is with most families with small children, but having the family together and sharing our day has become important to all of us.

Infants should be fed early, which makes our dinnertime a time when we can concentrate on eating and not on feeding the baby. It is easiest to place the baby in a jumper chair or highchair when you eat dinner. We usually offer the baby some of our food or crackers, so that he feels part of the dining process. This way the baby gets to know and understand the dinnertime routine, and, once he is old enough, will want to participate in the dinnertime conversation. Dinnertime can be a truly wonderful family experience.

MEAT

Infants and small children should avoid pork, because it tends to be too rich for their digestive systems. Cook meat until it's tender but do not overcook, as this will toughen it and make it difficult to puree. Red meat should be cooked to an internal temperature of 150°F., poultry 160°F. Test with a meat thermometer.

Remove any fat, skin, bones, or cartilage and cut in small pieces. Place in a food mill, blender, or food processor. To thin, use ¼ cup of milk/formula, cooking juices, or stock for each cup of prepared meat. Cool the pureed meat mixture and freeze it in ice cube trays or small containers. One serving would consist of ½ cup of meat. Serve within 24 hours.

In all of our recipes, soy milk can be used in place of cow's milk; tofu can be used in place of meat; chicken should be free-range; and beef should be organically raised and hormone-free.

Meat Dinner

MAKES 1 CUP

½ cup cubed, cooked meat (lamb, beef, or chicken)
2 tablespoons cooked vegetables (carrots, squash, spinach, peas)
¼ cup cooked rice, potatoes, or noodles
½ cup milk, formula, or broth

Combine all the ingredients and blend in a food processor, food mill, or blender until smooth. Serve warm or at room temperature.

Recommended for ages 8 months+

Sweet Potato and Chicken Dinner

MAKES 1 TO 2 SERVINGS

1 sweet potato, scrubbed
¼ cup bite-size pieces cooked white chicken meat
1 ripe apricot, peeled and pitted
½ cup cooked brown rice (page 41)
½ cup formula or other liquid

Puncture the skin of the sweet potato with a fork or knife and microwave on High until soft, about 8 minutes. For conventional ovens, bake in a preheated 400°F. oven for 45 minutes.

When cool enough to handle, scoop out the meat of the sweet potato into a food processor, food mill, or blender. Add the chicken, apricot, brown rice, and ¼ cup of the formula. Blend until smooth. Add more formula until you achieve the desired consistency. Store leftovers in the refrigerator for no more than 2 days.

Recommended for ages 8 months+

Vegetable Beef Dinner

MAKES 1 TO 2 SERVINGS

1 cup water
¼ cup ¼-inch-thick carrot slices
¼ cup cooked lean meat
¼ cup cooked barley (page 41)
½ cup formula or other liquid

❀

Put the water in a saucepan with a steamer basket and bring to a boil. Put the carrots in the steamer basket and steam until tender, about 5 minutes.

Combine the carrots, meat, barley, and ¼ cup of the formula in a food processor, food mill, or blender, and process until they're smooth. Add more formula or liquid, as needed. Serve warm or at room temperature.

Recommended for ages 8 months+

Vegetable Turkey Dinner

¼ *cup sliced carrots*
½ *apple, peeled, cored and cut into wedges*
¼ *cup bite-size cooked turkey meat pieces*
½ *cup cooked barley (page 41)*
½ *cup formula*

Place the carrots and apple in a steamer and steam until soft, about 5 minutes.

Place the carrots, apples, turkey, barley, and ¼ cup of the formula in a food processor, food mill, or blender, and process until they're smooth. Add more formula, as needed. Serve warm or at room temperature. Store leftovers in the refrigerator for no more than 2 days.

Recommended for ages 8 months+

Potato and Green Bean Dinner

MAKES 1 TO 2 SERVINGS

1 cup water
1 potato, peeled and cut into bite-size pieces
¼ cup fresh or frozen cut green beans
¼ cup shredded Cheddar cheese
½ cup cooked brown rice (page 41)
½ cup formula

✿

Put the water in a saucepan with a steamer basket and bring to a boil. Add the potato pieces to the steamer basket and steam until soft, about 5 minutes.

Steam the green beans (fresh or frozen) until they're soft, 3 to 5 minutes.

Place the potato, beans, cheese, rice, and ¼ cup of the formula in a food processor, food mill, or blender, and process until smooth. Add more formula until you reach the desired consistency. Serve warm or at room temperature.

Recommended for ages 8 months+

Pasta Dinner

1 cup water
½ carrot, sliced ⅛ inch thick
¼ cup cut green beans
½ cup cooked pasta
1 fresh tomato, peeled, seeded, and cut up
¼ cup drained canned chick-peas
¼ cup formula

Put the water in a saucepan with a steamer basket and bring to a boil. Add the carrot and green beans to the steamer basket and steam until tender, about 5 minutes.

Combine the pasta, tomato, chick-peas, carrot, and green beans in a food processor, food mill, or blender, and process until they're smooth. Add the formula to the mixture 2 tablespoons at a time, and blend until smooth. Serve warm or at room temperature.

Recommended for ages 10 months+

Brown Rice and Lentil Dinner

MAKES 2 SERVINGS

1 cup water
¼ cup ⅛-inch-thick carrot slices
¼ cup ¼-inch-thick apple slices
½ cup cooked brown rice (page 41)
½ cup cooked lentils
½ cup formula

Put the water in a saucepan with a steamer basket and bring to a boil. Add the carrots and apple slices to the steamer basket and steam until tender, about 5 minutes.

Place the rice, lentils, carrots, apples, and ¼ cup of the formula in a food processor, food mill, or blender, and process until they're smooth. Add more formula until you have reached the desired consistency. Serve warm or at room temperature.

Recommended for ages 8 months+

pples and Chicken

MAKES 2 SERVINGS

1 cup water
½ cup sliced apples
½ cup shredded cooked white chicken
¼ cup brown rice (page 41)
½ cup formula

❖

Put the water in a saucepan with a steamer basket and bring to a boil. Add the apple slices to the steamer basket and steam until tender, about 5 minutes.

Combine the apple slices, chicken, rice, and ¼ cup of the formula in a food processor, food mill, or blender, and process until they're smooth. Add more liquid, as needed. Serve warm or at room temperature.

Recommended for ages 8 months+

The Well Fed Baby Dinner

roccoli and Chicken Dinner

1 cup water
½ cup broccoli florets
¼ cup shredded cooked white chicken
¼ cup cooked brown rice (page 41)
½ cup formula

Put the water in a saucepan with a steamer basket and bring to a boil. Add the broccoli to the steamer basket and steam until tender, about 5 minutes.

Place the broccoli, chicken, rice, and ¼ cup of the formula in a food processor, food mill, or blender, and process until they're smooth. Add more formula, as needed. Serve warm or at room temperature.

Recommended for ages 8 months+

Spaghetti and Beef Dinner

¼ cup lean ground beef
½ cup cooked spaghetti (angel hair pasta works well)
1 fresh tomato, peeled, seeded, and cut up

❀

Heat a skillet over medium-high heat. Add the ground beef and cook, stirring, until the meat is brown and crumbly.

Combine the beef, spaghetti, and tomato in a food processor, food mill, or blender, and process until the mixture is smooth or slightly chunky, depending on what consistency your baby can tolerate. Serve warm or at room temperature.

Recommended for ages 10 months+

Summer Vegetable Dinner

MAKES 4 SERVINGS

1 cup water
¼ cup ½-inch green bean pieces
¼ cup corn kernels
¼ cup ¼-inch zucchini slices
¼ small onion, sliced into ¼-inch wedges
¼ cup ¼-inch carrot slices
¼ cup drained canned chick-peas
½ cup cooked brown rice (page 41)
1 teaspoon almond butter (optional)
¼ cup formula

Put the water in a saucepan with a steamer basket and bring to a boil. Add the green beans, corn, zucchini, onion, and carrots to the steamer basket and steam until tender, about 5 minutes.

Place the steamed vegetables, chick-peas, rice, almond butter (if using), and 2 tablespoons of the formula in a food processor, food mill, or blender, and process until they're smooth. Add more formula as needed. Serve warm or at room temperature.

Recommended for ages 8 months+

Whipped Corn Potatoes

MAKES 4 SERVINGS

3 large baking potatoes, peeled and cut into ½-inch pieces
1 cup formula or milk
2 tablespoons unsalted butter
Kernels from 2 ears cooked sweet corn

Place the potatoes in a large covered saucepan and cover with water. Bring to a boil over high heat. Lower the heat to medium-low and simmer until tender, about 30 minutes.

When the potatoes are done, remove from the heat and drain well. Place in the bowl of a mixer and add the formula and butter. Whip until the potatoes are smooth. Add the corn and puree. Serve warm or at room temperature.

Recommended for ages 10 months+. You may need to strain for younger infants.

Pea Custard

Chef-instructor John Jensen, California Culinary Academy

MAKES 4 SERVINGS

1½ cups mashed or pureed fresh or frozen (and thawed) peas
2 tablespoons butter or margarine, melted
3 large eggs, well beaten

✿

Preheat the oven to 300°F. Lightly grease 1 large or 4 individual custard molds. In a bowl, combine all the ingredients well.

Pour into the prepared mold(s). Set the mold(s) into a pan filled with water that comes halfway up the sides of the mold(s).

Place the pan in the oven and bake until a paring knife inserted into the center of the mold(s) comes out clean, about 30 minutes. Serve warm or at room temperature.

Recommended for ages 10 months+

Mashed Turnips

Chef-instructor John Jensen, California Culinary Academy

MAKES 4 SERVINGS

1 pound white or yellow turnips
Pinch of salt
¼ cup (½ stick) butter or margarine

Wash, pare, and slice the turnips.

Place the sliced turnips in a generous amount of boiling water and cook until they're soft, about 8 minutes, adding the salt just before the cooking is completed.

Drain and mash the turnips in the same pan, then place the pan, uncovered, over a low heat for 10 minutes to dry the turnips. Stir the turnips regularly while drying them so they do not scorch or burn. Stir in the butter. Serve warm or at room temperature.

Recommended for ages 7 months+

Noodles and Chicken

MAKES 6 SERVINGS

1 tablespoon olive oil
½ pound mushrooms, sliced
2 tablespoons instant dry milk
1½ tablespoons cornstarch
2 teaspoons low-salt instant chicken broth
½ teaspoon minced fresh onion
Pinch of grated nutmeg
2 cups cold water
3 cups broad noodles, cooked according to package instructions and drained
3 cups 2-inch cooked chicken or turkey pieces
2 tablespoons grated Romano cheese

Preheat the oven to 350°F. Heat the olive oil in a skillet over medium-high heat; add the mushrooms and cook, stirring, until tender, 5 to 10 minutes.

Combine the dry milk, cornstarch, instant chicken broth, onion, and nutmeg with the cold water in a large saucepan. Cook over medium heat until the mixture thickens and bubbles for 1 minute.

Arrange the noodles in an 8-cup baking dish. Spread the mushrooms over the noodles; top with the chicken. Pour the sauce over, then sprinkle with the cheese.

Bake the casserole until it's bubbly, about 30 minutes. Puree in a food processor, food mill, or blender until it's smooth. Serve warm or at room temperature.

Recommended for ages 10 months+

The Well Fed Baby Dinner

$\int$ada's **Stuffed Zucchini**

4 zucchini, cut in half lengthwise
6 tablespoons canola or olive oil
2 onions, chopped
2 green peppers, seeded and chopped
1 pound lean ground chuck
½ teaspoon dried oregano

Preheat the oven to 350°F. Plunge the zucchini halves into a pot of boiling water and cook until tender, 8 to 10 minutes. Drain, scoop out the center pulp to make boats, and retain the pulp. Discard any large seeds.

In a skillet, heat the oil over medium-high heat, add the onions and peppers, and cook, stirring, until the onions are golden brown, 5 to 7 minutes. Add the meat and cook, stirring, until browned, about 10 minutes. Stir in the oregano and zucchini pulp.

Place the zucchini boats in 2 large baking pans. Spoon the hamburger mixture into them. Bake for 45 to 60 minutes, until the tops of the boats are brown. Scoop out the contents of the zucchini boats, including all of the zucchini flesh, and transfer to a food processor, food mill, or blender. Puree until you achieve the desired consistency. Restuff them for serving. Serve warm or at room temperature.

Recommended for ages 10 months+

Yogurt Potatoes

1 large baking potato
2 tablespoons chopped cooked broccoli
2 tablespoons grated Cheddar cheese
2 tablespoons nonfat plain yogurt

Preheat the oven to 400°F.

Prick the potato with a fork in several places, then bake it until tender, about 1 hour.

Split the baked potato in half and scoop out the cooked potato. Fill the potato shell with the broccoli, cheese, and potato, and bake for another 10 minutes.

Place the yogurt and baked ingredients in a food processor, food mill, or blender, and process until they are smooth. You may need to add more yogurt for the desired consistency. Serve warm or at room temperature.

Recommended for ages 8 months+

6

❀

The
Well Fed Baby
Soups

SOUPS ARE SUCH A BASIC KIND OF DISH THAT THEY CAN be offered at lunch and dinner. At lunchtime, you can add a piece of fruit, and you have a well-balanced meal. Children, especially, enjoy soups that are filled with multicolored pastas or alphabet pasta. Soups offer a multitude of taste experiences, which is why they are the subject of this chapter.

The following are adult-size servings.

In all of our recipes, soy milk can be used in place of cow's milk; tofu can be used in place of meat; chicken should be free-range; and beef should be organically raised and hormone-free.

Chicken Stock

Executive chef Suzette Gresham-Tognetti, Ristorante Acquerello

MAKES 4 SERVINGS

One 4½-pound chicken
4 quarts cold water
1 onion, peeled
2 large carrots, peeled
3 to 4 stalks celery
1 bay leaf
1 clove garlic
½ teaspoon fresh or dried thyme (optional)
¼ bunch fresh parsley sprigs

Wash the chicken. Remove any internal parts remaining in the body cavity. Place the chicken into a deep pot and cover with the cold water.

Turn the flame to high. Skim and discard any foam that rises to the surface. Lower the heat to medium and add the remaining ingredients. Maintain the pot at a simmer, skimming the surface occasionally. Allow to cook until the chicken is falling-off-the-bone tender and the liquid seems reduced by about one third of the original amount, about 30 minutes.

(continued)

Remove from the heat. Gently pour off a portion of the chicken stock, while passing through a medium strainer.

Transfer the chicken to a serving platter or ovenproof dish. Finish straining the remainder of the broth. Reserve the strained-out vegetables to puree with chicken for baby.

Pour the entire quantity of broth through a fine strainer (tea strainer, cheesecloth, etc.) into a container suitable for the refrigerator or freezer.

Recommended for ages 10 months+

Note: It is easy to produce a quality meal for the entire family, including your infant.

As a chef, at home the last thing that I want to do is fuss unnecessarily over the stove — so it's one-pot cooking for me! Some of the best foods are the simplest.

This recipe yields "chicken stock," but the idea is not to stop there. Try multiplying the yield of your efforts by first serving the whole boiled chicken that evening and either serving the broth with pastina (tiny pasta) to your infant or perhaps whipping some quick-cooking polenta with it.

The blender, food processor, or food mill could be considered a key appliance here. Simply by dropping a chunk of chicken and vegetables from the broth into the blender and pureeing, you'll have baby food of the highest quality.

Savory Noodle Soup

Chef Martin Yan, Yan Can Cook

MAKES 4 SERVINGS

1 pound egg noodles
5 cups chicken stock (page 139)
1 teaspoon peeled and minced fresh ginger
½ cup julienned ham
2 cups finely chopped spinach leaves, tough stems removed
4 teaspoons soy sauce

In a pot, cook the noodles according to the package instructions. Drain, rinse under cold running water, and drain again.

In another pot, bring the stock, ginger, and ham to a boil over medium-high heat. Reduce the heat to medium-low and simmer for 2 minutes.

Place the noodles in a deep soup bowl. Place the spinach on top of the noodles, sprinkle with soy sauce, and pour the hot broth over all. Puree or chop in a food processor or blender until you have the desired consistency. Serve warm or at room temperature.

Recommended for ages 10 months+

Alphabet Soup

Executive chef Reimund Pitz, Epcot Center Foods

MAKES 4 SERVINGS

1½ cups chicken stock (page 139)
1½ cups beef stock
¼ cup diced carrot
¼ cup peeled and diced rutabaga
¼ cup diced celery
¼ cup diced onion
1 cup crushed canned tomatoes
¼ cup frozen peas
¼ cup frozen cut green beans
2 tablespoons cooked pearl barley, cooled (page 41)
¼ cup alphabet noodles, cooked according to package instructions and cooled

In a 4-quart soup pot, combine the chicken and beef stocks. Bring to a boil and add the carrot, rutabaga, celery, and onion. Reduce the heat to medium and simmer until the vegetables are tender but not mushy, about 15 minutes.

Add the tomatoes, peas, and green beans. Simmer for an additional 5 minutes, then add the pearl barley and alphabet noodles. Heat only long enough to warm all the ingredients. Puree in a food processor or blender. Serve immediately.

Recommended for ages 8 months+

Riso e Patate (Rice and Potato Soup)

Chef-owner Lidia Bastianich, Felidia Ristorante (Reprinted by permission from La Cucina di Lidia.)

MAKES 4 SERVINGS

3 tablespoons olive oil
2 potatoes, peeled and cut into ¼-inch dice
2 carrots, shredded
2 stalks celery, halved
2 teaspoons tomato paste
10 cups chicken stock (page 139)
2 bay leaves
1 cup long-grain rice

In a deep pot or large saucepan, heat the olive oil over medium-high heat. Add the potatoes and cook, turning occasionally, until they're browned, about 5 minutes. Add the carrots and celery, and cook for 2 to 3 minutes over medium heat, stirring with a wooden spoon. Add the tomato paste, stock, and bay leaves. Cover the pot and simmer for 40 minutes over medium-low heat.

Add the rice and cook until it's tender, 12 minutes longer. Remove the celery and bay leaves. Puree or chop in a food processor or blender. Serve warm or at room temperature.

Recommended for ages 8 months+

Vegetable Stock

Chef Tracy Pikhart Ritter (Reprinted by permission from Stamina Cuisine.)

MAKES 6 TO 7 CUPS

1 tablespoon olive oil
2 large onions, chopped
3 large carrots, sliced
2 stalks celery, sliced
1 medium-size potato, peeled and chopped
4 summer squash (zucchini or yellow), chopped
3 tomatoes, peeled, seeded, and chopped
½ cup dried white beans
1 bay leaf
¼ cup parsley stems
2 quarts cold water

Heat the oil in a stockpot over medium-high heat; add the onions and cook, stirring, until soft, about 5 minutes. Add the carrots, celery, potato, squash, and tomatoes and cook, stirring, for 15 minutes over medium-low heat. Add the remaining ingredients, bring to a boil, reduce the heat to medium-low, and simmer until the beans are tender, about 1 hour. Strain through a cheesecloth. Serve warm or at room temperature.

Recommended for ages 8 months+

$\int$weet Potato Soup

Executive chef. Bernd W. Liebergesell. Westin St. Francis Hotel

MAKES 4 SERVINGS

2 tablespoons unsalted butter or margarine
½ cup finely chopped onion
1 cup finely chopped leeks (white part only and well washed)
1 large clove garlic, minced
3 large carrots, thinly sliced
1 bay leaf
1½ pounds large sweet potatoes, peeled and cut into ¼-inch cubes
¾ pound russet potatoes, cut into ¼-inch cubes
6 cups chicken stock (page 139)
2 cups water

In a large stockpot, melt the butter over medium heat, add the onion, leeks, garlic, carrots, and bay leaf and cook, stirring, until softened.

Add the potatoes, chicken stock, and water and simmer until everything is soft, 25 to 30 minutes. Discard the bay leaf.

In a blender or food processor, puree the soup in small batches until it's very smooth. Serve warm or at room temperature.

Recommended for ages 8 months+

Carrot Soup

Executive chef Patrizio Sacchetto, Umberto's

MAKES 4 SERVINGS

¼ cup (½ stick) butter or margarine
2 yellow onions, finely chopped
1¼ pounds carrots, finely diced
2½ cups chicken stock (page 139)
3 tablespoons medium or long-grain rice
¾ to 1 cup milk

In a medium-size, heavy saucepan, melt 2 tablespoons of the butter. Add the onions and carrots and cook over low heat for about 10 minutes.

Add the stock and rice to the saucepan and bring to a boil. Reduce the heat to low, cover, and cook until the carrots and rice are very tender, about 30 minutes.

Transfer the carrots, rice, and the cooking juices to a blender or food processor and puree until they're smooth. Return to the saucepan and simmer, uncovered, over low heat, stirring often, for 5 minutes.

Add ¾ cup of the milk and bring the soup to a boil. If the soup is too thick, stir in the remaining milk. (The soup can be kept, covered, up to 2 days in the refrigerator. If necessary, reheat the soup over medium-low heat, stirring.)

Stir in the remaining 2 tablespoons of butter. Puree in a food processor to remove any lumps or until the soup is smooth. Serve warm or at room temperature.

Recommended for ages 10 months+

Minestra di Funghi Selvatici (Wild Mushroom Soup)

Chef-owner Lidia Bastianich, Felidia Ristorante (Reprinted by permission from La Cucina di Lidia.)

MAKES 6 SERVINGS

8 pieces (⅔ ounce) dried porcini mushrooms
1½ cups warm water
5 tablespoons olive oil
1 medium-size onion, chopped
2 medium-size potatoes, peeled and cut into ¼-inch cubes
2 medium-size carrots
1 large shallot, chopped
2½ quarts chicken stock (page 139)

Soak the mushrooms in the water until softened, about 20 minutes. Drain, reserving all but the last 2 teaspoons of the steeping liquid (to avoid unwanted sediments). Remove and rinse the softened porcini.

In a 5-quart pot, heat the olive oil over medium heat, then add the onion and cook, stirring, until it's translucent, about 3 minutes. Add the potatoes, carrots, and shallot and cook for 2 minutes, stirring occasionally. Add the stock, drained porcini, and reserved soaking liquid, and bring to a boil. Reduce the heat and keep at a low boil until the vegetables are tender, about 10 minutes. Puree in a food processor or blender until smooth. Serve warm or at room temperature.

Recommended for ages 8 months+

Garden Vegetable Soup

MAKES 6 SERVINGS

2 medium-size potatoes, cut into ½-inch cubes
2 medium-size carrots, cut into ¼-inch slices
1 cup diced string beans
1 medium-size onion, diced
2 medium-size summer squash (yellow or zucchini), cut into ¼-inch slices
2 large stalks celery, cut into ¼-inch slices
3 medium-size tomatoes, peeled, seeded, and cut into small pieces
¼ large green pepper, seeded and cut into ¼-inch strips
½ teaspoon minced fresh garlic
½ cup pearl barley, brown rice, or whole-wheat pasta

Place the vegetables in a large saucepan and add enough water to cover them completely. Bring to a boil and add the garlic. Simmer over medium heat until the vegetables are nearly tender, about 15 minutes.

Add the barley and continue to cook until it's tender. Puree in a food processor or blender. Serve warm.

Recommended for ages 8 months+

Beef and Bean Soup

MAKES 8 SERVINGS

2 tablespoons butter or margarine
1 pound lean steak, cut into ¼-inch pieces
One 28-ounce can whole tomatoes, drained
1 cup beef stock
1 cup water
½ cup barley
¼ cup chopped onion
1 small package frozen lima beans
1 small package frozen Italian or green beans
One 8-ounce can butter beans, drained

Melt the butter in a skillet over medium-high heat. Add the steak and cook, stirring, until it's browned on all sides, about 10 minutes.

Stir in the tomatoes, stock, water, barley, and onion. Bring to a boil, reduce the heat to medium, and let simmer for 50 minutes.

Stir in the lima beans and green beans. Bring to a boil, reduce the heat to medium, cover, and simmer for 10 minutes.

Stir in the butter beans. Cover and simmer for 10 minutes. Puree the soup in a food processor or blender. Serve warm.

Recommended for 8 months+

Quick and Delicious Split Pea Soup

MAKES 4 CUPS

1 cup dried split peas, rinsed and picked over
3¼ cups water
1 cup chopped onion
1 cup chopped celery
1¼ cups sliced carrots

Place the peas, water, onion, and celery in a medium-size pot, bring just to a boil, then reduce the heat to low, cover, and simmer for 40 minutes.

Put the soup in a food processor or blender and puree until smooth. Then add the sliced carrots and blend briefly, just enough to have bits of carrot in the soup (unless you want it totally smooth). Return the soup to the pot and cook for another 10 minutes. Serve warm or at room temperature.

Recommended for ages 8 months+

Lentil Chicken Soup

2 tablespoons butter or margarine
1 small onion, thinly slivered
¼ cup finely chopped celery
¼ cup finely chopped parsley
1 medium-size carrot, shredded
½ cup dried lentils, rinsed and drained
3 cups chicken stock (page 139)

In a 2- to 3-quart saucepan over medium heat, melt the butter. Add the onion, celery, parsley, and carrot and cook, stirring often, until the vegetables are soft but not browned, 5 to 8 minutes. Add the lentils and stock.

Bring the soup to a boil, cover, and reduce the heat to medium. Stirring occasionally so the lentils don't stick to the bottom, simmer until the lentils are tender, 25 to 30 minutes.

Puree in a food processor or blender and serve warm or at room temperature.

Recommended for ages 8 months+

Potato Soup

5 medium-size leeks
2 tablespoons butter or margarine
1 small onion, finely chopped
3 medium-size potatoes, peeled and cut into ½-inch dice
4 cups boiling water
3 cups milk

Cut off the root ends and tops of the leeks. Clean, drain, and slice them about ¼ inch thick.

In a 3- to 4-quart saucepan over medium heat, melt the butter. Add the leeks and onion and cook, stirring often, until they're soft but not browned, about 5 minutes. Mix in the pototoes and boiling water. Bring to a boil, cover, reduce the heat slightly, and cook until the potatoes are very tender, 25 to 30 minutes.

Puree the mixture, in 2 or 3 batches, in a blender or food processor, until the soup is smooth. Return to the cooking pan and stir in the milk. Stir over medium heat until steaming hot. Cover and refrigerate for 3 to 5 hours or overnight. Before serving, gently reheat in a saucepan over medium heat until warm.

Recommended for ages 10 to 12 months+

Nikolai's Borscht

2 carrots, sliced
1½ cups shredded raw beets
1 turnip, peeled and diced
1 medium-size onion, sliced
1 cup water
2 tablespoons cider vinegar
6 cups beef stock
2 cups diced cooked beef
½ small cabbage, shredded

Combine the carrots, beets, the turnip, onion, water, and vinegar in a 2- to 3-quart saucepan. Bring to a boil, then reduce the heat to medium, cover, and simmer for 20 minutes. Add the stock, beef, and cabbage and simmer until all the vegetables are tender, 10 to 15 minutes.

Puree in a food processor or blender and serve warm or at room temperature.

Recommended for ages 8 months+

Minestrone

1 cup dried white beans
11 cups water
2 tablespoons olive oil
2 ⅓ to 3 pounds beef shanks, sliced ¾ to 1 inch thick
2 large onions, slivered
2 large carrots, chopped
2 stalks celery, thinly sliced
2 cloves garlic, minced or pressed
½ cup chopped fresh parsley
1 ham hock
One 28-ounce can whole tomatoes, coarsely chopped
1 medium-size turnip, peeled and diced
2 cups chopped Swiss chard leaves, tough stems removed
½ cup fresh or frozen peas
1½ cups hot cooked rice
2 cups shredded cabbage

Place the beans in a large bowl and add 3 cups of the water. Cover and let stand for at least 8 hours; drain, discarding the soaking liquid. (Or, to shorten the soaking period, place the beans in a 2- to 3-quart pan with 4 cups water, bring to a boil, and boil briskly, uncovered, for 2 minutes. Remove from the heat, cover, and let stand for 1 hour. Drain, discarding the soaking liquid.)

In a 7- to 8-quart kettle, heat the olive oil over medium heat. Add the beef shanks and brown on all sides, about 10 minutes. As you turn the shanks to brown the last side, add the onions; cook, stirring occasionally, until the onions are limp, about 10 minutes more.

Add the carrots, celery, garlic, parsley, ham hock, tomatoes along with their liquid, soaked beans, and the remaining 8 cups of water. Bring to a boil, cover, reduce the heat to medium, and simmer until the meat and beans are tender, 3½ to 4 hours. Skim and discard any surface fat.

Remove the beef shanks and ham hock with a slotted spoon. When cool enough to handle, discard the bones and skin. Return the beef and ham in large chunks to the soup.

Add the turnip to the soup and simmer over medium heat, uncovered, for 10 minutes. Mix in the chard and peas and cook for 3 minutes more. Blend in the rice and cabbage and cook, stirring occasionally, just until the cabbage is wilted and bright green, 3 to 5 minutes. Puree in a food processor or blender. Serve warm or at room temperature.

Recommended for 10 to 12 months+

Noodles and Bean Soup

MAKES 12 SERVINGS

1 pound dried pinto beans
½ cup olive oil
1½ cups chopped onions
3 tablespoons minced garlic
3 bay leaves
One 6-ounce can tomato paste
One 28-ounce can tomato puree
10 cups water
1 cup favorite small pasta noodles

Cover the beans with cold water to cover and soak overnight.

Heat the olive oil in a large soup pot. Add the onions, garlic, and bay leaves and cook over low heat, stirring occasionally, until the onions and garlic are soft and translucent, 10 to 15 minutes.

Add the tomato paste and puree and cook for another 5 mintues. Stir in the water, cover partially, and cook over medium heat for 20 minutes.

Drain the beans and add them to the soup pot. Reduce the heat to medium-low, cover, and simmer until the beans are tender, about 1½ hours.

(continued)

Add the pasta and continue to simmer until the pasta is tender, another 10 minutes. Remove the bay leaves. Puree or chop in a food processor or blender to desired consistency. Serve warm or at room temperature.

Recommended for ages 10 months+

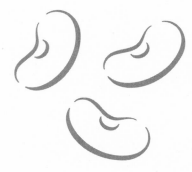

7

The Well Fed
Baby Snacks
and Desserts

ASMALL CHILD WHO CANNOT EAT MUCH AT MEALTIME may need to snack. Snacks should not be junk food but should contribute to your baby's nutrition. Snacks need not be fancy but should be nutritious and delicious.

Children should be served their snack, be allowed to eat it, and then be finished eating until the next meal. If they are allowed to eat from the cupboards and refrigerator at will, they may turn the day into one continuous snack period. Meals can have little meaning and many medical and weight problems may result.

Remember that your child will want the same foods that you eat. Choose snacks that are good for your health. You can make healthy snacks from foods that you have around the house.

In all of our recipes, soy milk can be used in place of cow's milk; tofu can be used in place of meat; chicken should be free-range; and beef should be organically raised and hormone-free.

Some good snacks are:

BABIES 6 TO 8 MONTHS:

Mashed soft cooked vegetables

Cottage cheese

Graham or unsalted soda crackers

Ripe banana

Toast strips

Plain bread sticks

Fruit juice, fruit shake, or yogurt drink

Fruit Popsicles

Zwieback

Whole bagel

BABIES 9 TO 12 MONTHS:

Soft cooked vegetables

Peaches, apples, pears, apricot, papaya, bananas—raw or canned, peeled, pitted, and cut into small pieces

Soft cheese

Hamburger, broken into small pieces, or tiny meatballs

Egg yolk

Strips of tender beef or chicken, cut into small pieces

Cottage cheese

Water-packed canned tuna

Toast

Yogurt

Cubes of cooked potato

Toasted whole-grain waffle, cut into small pieces

Dry unsweetened cereal (like Cheerios) with milk

Graham crackers, oatmeal cookies

Fruit juice

Cheese cubes

Quick breads such as banana or pumpkin, cut into small pieces

Pretzels

Rice cakes

Banana sandwich

Melted cheese on toast

Tofutti

3 ounces soft tofu
¼ banana, peeled
¼ peach, peeled and pitted

Puree all the ingredients in a food processor or blender.
Pour into small plastic containers and freeze until semi-soft, like ice cream.

Recommended for ages 8 months+

Rice Pudding

2 cups cooked brown rice (page 41)
2 cups milk
½ cup dry milk
¼ cup firmly packed brown sugar
1 tablespoon margarine, melted
2 large eggs, beaten
½ teaspoon pure vanilla extract
Plain bread crumbs or wheat germ

❀

Preheat the oven to 350°F.

In a mixing bowl, mix all the ingredients together except the bread crumbs.

Grease a 1-quart ovenproof casserole dish and sprinkle the bottom with bread crumbs. Pour in the pudding mixture and sprinkle more crumbs on top. Bake until a knife inserted in the center comes out clean, 20 minutes. Serve cold.

Recommended for ages 8 months+

Mixed Berries and Yogurt Mold

Executive chef Rick Pestana, Epcot Center Foods

MAKES 2 SERVINGS

1 cup natural nonfat strawberry yogurt
1 cup pureed blueberries and raspberries
1 teaspoon unflavored gelatin
2 tablespoons boiling water

Coat two 3- or 3 ½-inch cookie cutters with vegetable oil in the inside rim. Set the cookie cutters in the middle of a dinner plate and set in the refrigerator to cool.

Combine the yogurt and berries in a bowl. Dissolve the gelatin in the boiling water, then add to the yogurt and berries; mix well. Fill the cookie cutters with the yogurt mixture and place in the refrigerator to set, about 35 to 40 minutes. When ready to serve, pull the cookie cutters from the plate.

Recommended for ages 10 months+

Summer Berry Gelatin

Chef Jennifer Hoolhorst, American Institute of Wine and Food

MAKES 6 SERVINGS

1 envelope unflavored gelatin
2 cups Kerns strawberry nectar (grocery store, juice section)
1½ cups fresh raspberries, blackberries, or boysenberries, pureed

In a bowl, mix the gelatin with ½ cup of the cold juice. Heat the remaining juice in a saucepan just until it reaches a boil. Combine the hot juice and gelatin mixture. Chill the mixture until it thickens to the consistency of unbeaten egg whites.

Meanwhile, place ¼ cup of the pureed berries into each of 6 dessert dishes. When the gelatin is thickened, give it a stir (the juice may have separated) and pour it over the pureed berries. Chill until firm.

Recommended for ages 10 months+

Baked Banana Pudding

Chef Bernd W. Liebergesell, Westin St. Francis Hotel

MAKES 4 SERVINGS

⅓ cup sugar
2 tablespoons all-purpose unbleached flour
2 large eggs
⅔ cup milk
2 teaspoons pure vanilla extract
1 large banana, cut into ¼-inch slices

Preheat the oven to 400°F.

In a blender, mix together the sugar, flour, eggs, milk, and vanilla. Blend until smooth.

Butter a small casserole dish and layer the sliced bananas in it. Pour the blended pudding mixture over the bananas and bake until the mixture is firm, 20 to 25 minutes.

Recommended for ages 10 months+

Banana Ice Cream

Executive chef Amy Ferguson-Ota, Ritz Carlton Mauna Lai

MAKES 4 SERVINGS

6 very ripe bananas

❁

Peel the bananas and freeze until firm.

You will need a strong juicer or extractor. Process the bananas as you would any juice. They will come out a creamy, icelike frozen banana dessert.

Recommended for ages 8 months+

Fruit Custard

¼ cup fruit puree (banana, peach, or pear)
1 egg yolk, beaten
¼ cup milk

Preheat the oven to 350°F.

In a bowl, blend the ingredients together. Pour into 2 custard cups and place in a pan of water, with the water coming a ½ inch up the sides of the custard cups.

Bake until a knife comes out clean when inserted into the center of the custard, about 30 minutes. Will keep in the refrigerator up to 3 days.

Recommended for ages 10 months+

Frozen Fruit Pops

MAKES 5 SERVINGS

1 pound bag of frozen fruit, thawed
¾ cup juice of choice (apple, pear, or cherry)

Pour the fruit and juice into a blender or food processor and blend until the fruit and juice look like a smooth, thick soup.

Fill 5-ounce paper cups with the fruit mixture to ¼ inch below the top and place in the freezer.

After 1 hour, when the fruit mixture should be partially frozen, put a plastic or wooden stick into the center of each cup. Return the cups to the freezer. In about 3 hours, the fruit mixture should be completely frozen.

Take a cup out and warm it between your hands until the pop can be pulled out of the cup by the handle.

Recommended for ages 8 months+

Pretzel Crisps

MAKES 12

1 cup warm water
1 envelope active yeast
1 tablespoon sugar
2½ cups all-purpose unbleached flour
1 large egg yolk, beaten

Preheat the oven to 425°F. Grease a cookie sheet.

In a bowl, mix the water, yeast, and sugar together and set aside for 15 minutes. Add the flour and knead for 5 minutes.

Cut the dough into small pieces and roll the pieces into ropes. Twist the ropes into the traditional pretzel shapes and place on the cookie sheet. Brush the tops with the beaten egg.

Bake for 15 to 20 minutes, until the pretzels are golden brown. Offer stale or frozen.

Note: For Quick and Easy Pretzels, make this recipe with thawed, storebought frozen bread dough.

Recommended for ages 10 months+

Yogurt Fruit Crunch

MAKES 4 SERVINGS

2 cups nonfat plain yogurt
1 cup granola cereal
1 cup pureed fruit

Spoon layers of the yogurt, cereal, and fruit into 4 individual bowls and serve.

Recommended for ages 10 months+

Yum's Yogurt

1 cup peeled, seeded, and diced fruit
¼ cup frozen apple juice concentrate
1 cup nonfat plain yogurt

Process all the ingredients together in a food processor or blender until smooth and serve.

Recommended for ages 7 months+

Tofu Custard

3 large eggs
1 cup firm tofu
2 tablespoons rice malt sweetener (located in the specialty food section of grocery)
1 cup milk
1 teaspoon pure vanilla extract
½ teaspoon ground cinnamon

Preheat the oven to 350°F. Lightly butter a 1½-quart casserole dish.

Beat the eggs in a medium-size bowl.

In a blender or food processor, process the tofu, sweetener, milk, vanilla, and cinnamon together until they're smooth. Pour the blended mixture into the bowl with the beaten eggs and stir, mixing well.

Pour the custard mixture into the buttered casserole dish. Bake for 1 hour, until the top is light brown, or, when a knife is inserted in the middle, it comes out clean. Let cool and serve at room temperature.

Recommended for ages 8 months+

Tips for Eating Out with the Well Fed Baby

After a busy day, cooking is not the first item on your agenda. We have a few suggestions for taking your baby and/or child out for dinner.

1. Fast-food restaurants cater specifically to children, because they offer not only food but placemats to color, monkey bars, swings, slides, and rides that will keep children occupied while you finish eating. Many offer fresh vegetables or salad bars.

2. Ethnic dining can be a treat for children, because many ethnic restaurants are especially tolerant of children and also offer wonderful amenities. Many ethnic foods such as poo-poo platters, quesadillas, pot stickers, tempura, and noodle dishes really appeal to the young diner.

3. Talk to the chef, manager, or server. Usually they can arrange to have the sauce left off a particular dish, served on the side, or reduce/eliminate hot spices.

4. Dining at off-peak hours or early in the evening is usually your best bet, as the young diner often receives special attention from the staff. Also, young diners are usually at their best in the early evening.

5. Refrain from ordering multicourse meals, or, if you do, make sure that the waiter brings the children's entrées when the first course is served to the adults.

6. Be sure to ask if there are highchairs or booster seats. Parents should ask if they can bring a stroller into a restaurant.

7. Parents should set realistic goals for their children's behavior. Lay down a few ground rules before you get to the restaurant.

8. Tuck suction-cup toys, rattles, and pacifiers into a pocket or purse, and consider packing a snack.

9. If the child does act up, escort the child from the table out of the dining room or restaurant. There is nothing worse for diners than to have a child pitch a fit in a restaurant while they may have paid for a sitter to stay home with their children. Remain with the upset child in the rest room, lounge area, or outside until she gets her act together.

10. You can entertain your child with a bowl of chipped ice.

11. Ask for a package of crackers right away.

12. Grilled cheese and baked potatoes are popular with children.

13. If you order soup, you can spoon out the vegetables and meat for baby.

14. Bring a garlic press with you. It can mince up food very nicely.

15. Tell the wait staff that you want to order right away.

16. Feed a snack or small meal to the child prior to going out, because sometimes it can be a long wait before being served.

17. Always be prepared.

18. Leave a fair tip: 15 to 20 percent. The staff will welcome you back!

The Contributing Chefs

The following chefs contributed their time and recipes to the compilation of this cookbook. Although some of the recipes were not included, we would like to thank them all for their time and effort by mentioning them and their place of business.

Chef-owner Lidia Bastianich
Felidia Ristorante
243 East 58th Street
New York, NY 10022

Executive chef Phyllis Bologna
National Accounts Development
General Foods USA Foodservice Division
250 North Street EG3
White Plains, NY 10625

Chef and author Flo Braker
1441 Edgewood Drive
Palo Alto, CA 94301

Chef Dennis Clews, CWPC CEC
Stanford Park Hotel
100 El Camino Real
Menlo Park, CA 94025

Chef-owner Bert Cutino
Executive chef Karl Ilie Staub
Sardine Factory
701 Wave Street
Monterey, CA 93940

Executive chef Roger Dikon
Makena Resort
5400 Makena Alanui
Kihei, HI 96753

Chef and author Dean Fearling
The Mansion on Turtle Creek
2821 Turtle Creek Boulevard
Dallas, TX 75219

Amy Ferguson-Ota
Oodles of Noodles
75-1027 Henry Street
No. 102
Kailua, Kona, HI 96740

Chef-instructor and author Bo Frieberg
California Culinary Academy
625 Polk Street
San Francisco, CA 94102

Corporate executive chef Roberto Gerometta
Nestlé Brands Foodservice Company
800 North Brand Boulevard
Glendale, CA 91203

Executive chef-owner, Suzette Gresham-Tognetti
Ristorante Acquerello
1722 Sacramento
San Francisco, CA 94109

Chef Jennifer Hoolhorst
Director of Programs
The American Institute of Wine and Food
1550 Bryant Street, Suite 700
San Francisco, CA 94103

Chef-instructor John T. Jensen
California Culinary Academy
625 Polk Street
San Francisco, CA 94102

Chef-owner Hubert Keller
Fleur De Lys
777 Sutter Street
San Francisco, CA 94109

Chef Keith Keogh, president of the American
Culinary Federation
Epcot Center Foods
Orlando, FL 32819

Chef-instructor Lars Kronmark
California Culinary Academy
625 Polk Street
San Francisco, CA 94102

Executive chef Bernd W. Liebergesell
The Westin St. Francis Hotel
335 Powell Street
San Francisco, CA 94102

Chef-owner Emil Moser
Emiles
545 South Second Street
San Jose, CA 95112

Chef-instructor Mial Parker
California Culinary Academy
625 Polk Street
San Francisco, CA 94102

Chef-owner Cindy Pawlcyn
Mustards Grill and Fog City Diner
180 Harbor Drive, Suite 100
Sausalito, CA 94965

Executive chef Rick Pestana
Epcot Center Foods
Orlando, FL 32819

Executive chef Reimund Pitz
Epcot Center Foods
Orlando, FL 32819

Chef and author Tracy Pikhart Ritter
Stamina Cuisine
San Diego, CA 92660

Executive chef Patrizio Sacchetto
Umberto's
141 Steuart Street
San Francisco, CA 94105

Executive chef–owner Charles Saunders
Eastside Oyster Bar & Grill
133 East Napa Street
Sonoma, CA 95476

Chef and instructor Nadar Sharkes
Norsman Restaurant and Diablo Valley College
Diablo, CA 94506

Chef Hans Wiegand
The Claremont Resort and Tennis Club
Ashby and Domingo Avenues
Oakland, CA 94623

Chef-instructor and author Kenneth C. Wolfe
P.O. Box 456
Lafayette, CA 94549

Chef, author, and TV personality
Martin Yan
Yan Can Cook
1064 G Shell Boulevard
Foster City, CA 94404

Index